AF428706

Anchor Your Self-Worth

EMBRACE YOUR WORTH
TO FLOURISH IN LIFE

JACQUELINE HIGGINS

Copyright © 2024 Jacqueline Higgins.

All rights reserved. No part of this book may be reproduced, stored, or transmitted by any means—whether auditory, graphic, mechanical, or electronic—without written permission of both publisher and author, except in the case of brief excerpts used in critical articles and reviews. Unauthorized reproduction of any part of this work is illegal and is punishable by law.

DEDICATION

This book is dedicated to my parents, Molly and Norman Higgins, for whom I will always be eternally grateful. I will always cherish the blessing of being witness to their 70-year love story. To my late father, who is an enduring light in my heart and soul. My father was a man who exemplified immeasurable strength and compassion in such a gentle and chivalrous manner. To my mother who is still an inspiration and ongoing mentor. She has taught me many of life's gifts including grace, and perseverance, and instilled in me the belief that I could achieve anything. I still marvel at her resilience, strength, and passion for life. Mark, my love, I appreciate and value the life we share and the gift of support and encouragement you so generously extend. We hold the same vision, to become better versions of ourselves, so we can better serve the world. Our love story has just begun.

It was my journey of self-development and reflection that allowed me to open my heart to sharing love again: a gift I'm honored to share with readers of this book.

FORWARD

When I was 30 years old, I was diagnosed with an illness that would change the direction of my life. Going from modeling, and being viewed as beautiful, to someone who looked in the mirror and saw a sickly and unattractive woman was beyond demoralizing. As shallow as it sounds, I could have dealt with my illness more easily if I didn't have to share it with the world.

One day, I was on the train going into Boston for yet another doctor's appointment and a group of kids pointed at me and made a cruel comment about the way I looked. The medication had made me bloated. My eyes were protruding, my skin was a mess. A far cry from my days as a model.

Sometimes, the reason doesn't matter as to why we're not whole. We've all experienced something that has brought us to our knees.

It took almost five years before my focus shifted to meeting a nice man, getting married, and having kids. My life plan in a nutshell.

Going through a dating service, I finally met someone who wined and dined me and made me feel special. Heck, he brought a red rose on the first date. It was pure intoxication. I was completely lost in the whirlwind of our short courtship, which should have led me to pause and ask, "Why?"

I married this man for all the wrong reasons–vulnerability, feeling insecure, not feeling pretty, not feeling worthy. I was easily seduced by having a man simply fawn over me.

Our divorce was inevitable. As I became stronger, my ex felt threatened and would try to knock me back down emotionally. There was a time that

I'll never forget. The cruelty of his comments had brought me to tears, and he stood there staring at me with his arms crossed with a look of complete triumph on his face.

The takeaway, over time, and it took time and some counseling sessions, was not bitterness or blame, but the hard realization that I had attracted the man he was, and he was simply trying to reclaim the woman he believed I was. This is not an excuse for his behavior, but a bitter pill of self-realization.

One would think this life lesson of needing to regroup after my illness would have sunk in, but it wasn't too long after my divorce that I met another man, a great guy. We lived together for almost five years and shared many wonderful memories. We traveled extensively and explored so many interesting places, but I often felt trapped … like my life was being defined by his interests, his friends, what was most important to him. The break-up was like a second divorce. Friends and family thought we shared the perfect life; while I often felt lonely and confused.

I started online dating. An interesting adventure on so many levels. It was at this point that I adopted behaviors shared by many women. Shared statements like–all the good men are taken–I can't be bothered to train a man at this point–or men aren't trustworthy–it's easier to live alone. Sound familiar?

After stumbling with another man completely unsuited, who I met online, I finally stopped. Stopped the frantic search to settle down before I was "too old." And I stopped selling myself short.

My self-awareness journey spanned several years and continues to this day. I attended numerous seminars focused on self-development, listened to endless podcasts, read psychology and personal development books and research studies, and interviewed people who shared the type of relationship I was seeking with men who seemed more ideal. Although I paused dating for quite some time, I never lost faith. The more I learned about myself the clearer it became that I needed to become the woman that my ideal man would be attracted to. I needed to raise my standards and become a better version of myself. Like attracts like.

A NOTE TO THE READER

Although we've never met, I think our paths have likely crossed. Perhaps not literally, but we've been searching for the same insights and answers.

My hope is that the lessons and stories in this book give you the inspiration to transform how you feel about yourself and opens your heart to sharing love again. This book encourages you, teaches you, to live from the inside out. Sharing love starts with self-love.

While we may have different life experiences and varying beliefs, I believe we all share the need to express and feel love. I celebrate you as you begin a journey of personal development on the path to cultivating deeper self-worth.

Transformative is the word I would use to describe the contentment and peace that is felt when you live authentically and understand yourself deeply. When we consciously define our North Star life becomes more stable. We define how we show up, where and with whom based on the values and virtues we have as our compass. Our self-worth guided by our North Star becomes our anchor. An unshakable strength that allows us to navigate life without losing ourselves. To take life lessons in stride and grow. To become a better version of ourselves so we can live more passionately.

We're all on this journey of personal growth together. I'd love to invite you to join our community and sign-up for my complementary newsletter by visiting selfworthfoundations.com.

Remember, self-worth is you anchor.

CONTENTS

EMBARKING ON THE PATH

Foundations in Journaling and Meditation

*What lies behind us and what lies
before us are tiny matters,
compared to what lies within us.*

- RALPH WALDO EMERSON

Do you remember a time, perhaps the first time, when you felt your self-worth? A time when you stepped into believing you're worthy. It's an interesting question as it likely takes you back to childhood. A time when you felt the world was your oyster and the possibilities for who and what you could become seemed endless.

Over time, our self-confidence and sense of worth can be chipped away whether by divorce, disappointments, career choices, hurtful relationships, or mistakes we've made throughout our life journey. Maybe you find yourself in an unhealthy or unfulfilling relationship, but you can't find the courage to leave. Or your divorce or hurtful relationship left a scar that doesn't seem to heal. In your heart-of-hearts you know your potential exceeds the career you've followed and the life you've been leading. The little girl who believed she could accomplish anything has become the woman who has lost touch with her deepest desires and soulful dreams.

There are many wonderful quotes that capture the "why" to embark on a journey of self-discovery, but Oprah's quote, "You don't become what you want, you become what you believe," perfectly captures the essence of self-discovery. If you don't believe you're worthy of unconditional love or leading a purpose-filled life that feeds your soul, it's unlikely you'll secure, yet alone, sustain this mindset either. ***Self-worth and authenticity define every aspect of life.***

If your inner light has dimmed or you feel disconnected from your authenticity, I'm so glad you're here. What I love about the journey of self-discovery is the impact it can have not only on your life but on those around you. Just imagine a life where you're not defined by outdated stereotypes and limiting beliefs, a life where you're able to embrace the beauty of who you've become. As a woman, I've listened to my inner voice of self-defeating criticism and acquiesced to limiting stereotypes. But I've now reclaimed my inner voice.

My path to self-worth, leading an authentic life, and enjoying unconditional love was messy and far from a straight line, which is why I chose to write this book. To share insights that will hopefully disrupt the hypnotic rhythm of social standards and simply moving through life to empowering you to authentically show up and define your next chapter based on *your self-worth*.

My intention in the pages of this book is to take you through a journey of self-discovery. To move you from following your ego and external influences that may not serve you to following your heart—a powerful shift that can bring more fulfillment and alignment to your life. Our souls are our true home. The words in this book are an invitation for you to be true to your soul.

Your path of self-discovery can be illuminated through different resources, one is journaling. Writing things down takes it out of our heads. An enlightening book, *The Artist's Way*[1], first introduced me to the power of journaling. Every coach I've worked with has reinforced why journaling is an important aspect to our growth. If this is new for you, you're in for a treat. Some of the benefits of journaling include improved mental health, increased self-confidence, boosted emotional intelligence, increased goal achievement, inspired creativity, and enhanced critical thinking skills. The blank pages filled with your deepest thoughts gives you permission to step back, to witness some of your conditioned belief systems. The daily practice of writing can give you clarity and help you to transform your life. Journaling helps to clear your mind. In today's busy world it can seem difficult to allocate time to simply be—to stop and think. Journaling gives us permission to pause and focus on our thoughts.

How should you begin? Like many things in life, it's a personal choice. One way may be to start with gratitude. Your journal can be a simple book or a leatherbound gift to your future self.

As adults, we learn in different ways … we're all unique. But one thing is universal. When we not only read but write things down, we retain more.

You'll find that I'll refer to your journal throughout this book. I've often marveled at my progress over time. Thoughts that kept me linked to my past rather than feeling empowered seem so distant. Journaling will help you to close the gap between where you are and where you want to be . . . or who you want to become. Journaling helps you to get beyond the noise and really delve deeper into your thoughts, fears, desires, dreams, goals … whatever calls to you.

In the following pages, you'll find *Reflection and Practice Tools*—time to roll-up your sleeves and really contemplate what speaks to you. It's helpful to pause and reflect on what you've read and what you felt and learned. The exercises will help you to discover the personal meaning of what was shared. Trust yourself fully as you read through this book and take what serves you and leave the rest. Perhaps it's not the right time for certain things … You'll know.

Two beautiful gifts for your soul are mindfulness and self-reflection. Meditation reduces stress, strengthens your overall health, improves sleep, increases self-awareness, and improves clarity and calmness of mind. In fact, the American Psychological Association acknowledges the mental and physical benefits of meditation. Mindful mediation changes our brain and biology in very positive ways. It helps us to be present and, in turn, to be grateful.

Consider meditation to be like a muscle that improves over time. Be patient with yourself. Create a space and time for self-reflection–you deserve this precious gift. Perhaps an area lit by candles and soothing aromas, away from distractions will prove helpful. If you'd like to try a guided meditation, perhaps try Dr. Joe Dispenza's YouTube[2] video on meditation. Initially, you may find you meditate for two minutes, then five and then twenty. Your mind will wander as it always does, but over time you'll find your focus becomes stronger. It's your progress that counts. Ultimately, you'll find a soothing value to your practice.

CHAPTER ONE

UNVEILING AUTHENTICITY

Embracing Your True Self and Living Boldly

*When you discover how much you're worth,
you'll stop giving people discounts.*

— JAY SHETTY

We all have what it takes to lead the life we choose. The problem many of us share is that we've been taught to focus on building our self-confidence and envisioning the success we aspire to realize. Perhaps we've spoken positive mantras, created vision boards and other suggested actions. All are important without question but miss the need for a strong foundation.

Think back on something you wanted badly. Maybe you thought, *If only this were to happen*, then everything in your life would fall into place. Maybe it was a job, a relationship, a new home, winning a marathon, whatever it was that gave you the sense of accomplishment you felt was real. It was an amazing moment that you wanted to share. This was your time. You felt worthy of praise; you achieved your goal. My question is whether it solved the problem of what was missing in your life.

Sometimes the hardest thing to recognize is that *we* might be our problem. If we want to change the situation, we must first change ourselves. What do I mean by that?

Self-worth is your foundation or anchor. Self-worth means that you value yourself. It's a deeply rooted belief that you are worthy … of love, of respect, of being authentically you. Our self-worth is an inside job; it's not defined or dependent on the external. This is important to really think about as self-confidence, for example, is an external demonstration or evaluation of your skills, abilities and traits. Self-confidence can be bolstered or shattered at times. Whereas self-worth, when cultivated, remains a solid foundation from which you define and live your authentic life.

You may be surprised to learn how many women struggle with self-worth. These women are CEOs, public figures, women who seem to have everything but still don't feel as if they're enough. Their accomplishments are driven by the need to achieve one more thing to feel worthy … one more adornment of beauty, a better job title, a few less pounds, volunteering more … but the feeling of emptiness that comes from a lack of self-worth still exists. The need to realize greater accolades becomes their driver … and these women lose themselves … their true selves over time. The tokens of success become their focus instead of enjoying an authentic life.

Self-confidence can be so fragile. Self-worth is foundational.

There are many words to describe how we feel about ourselves. It's understandable if they all start to blend. Understanding the concepts of self-worth, self-confidence, and self-esteem are what we'll focus our attention on rather than confusing the issue with all the other "self" words. So, let's define each more clearly.

Self-esteem is what we think and feel about ourselves based on external *and* internal measures. Think accomplishments, achievements, appearance, intelligence, and realizing your definition of success. All have played a role in developing your self-esteem.

Although confidence is tied to both self-esteem and self-worth, it's more a feeling of competence in a specific area. Maybe tennis is your thing. You've taken lessons, practiced, and now play a couple times a week and win matches! You've developed self-confidence in your playing abilities on the court.

On the other hand, self-worth is the value we place on ourselves for simply being who we are. It's our intrinsic value. In self-worth there is no comparison because the value is within us, not external. Self-worth is not about your accomplishments. It's not about your age or the title on your business card. It's not about the home you live in or the car you drive or even how you look. **Self-worth is your belief that you are enough, period.** Now that's a powerful statement. The life impact of having a strong sense of self-worth cannot be overstated. Reflect on the times you held yourself back from realizing a dream or underestimated your self-worth or compromised yourself in a relationship or career. There was a part of you that knew you were meant for more, but you lacked the deep sense of worth to help you navigate through self-doubt.

WHY SELF-WORTH IS SO IMPORTANT-
LET ME COUNT THE WAYS

- It allows you to love and respect yourself
- It helps you to make wiser decisions
- It supports healthier personal boundaries
- It enables you to be confident
- It empowers you to be authentic
- It supports living a healthier lifestyle
- It helps you to move away from toxic people and habits
- It inspires you to find loving friends and partners
- It improves the overall quality of your life

SELF-WORTH AND RELATIONSHIPS

The most important person you must be honest with about your self-worth is yourself. We've often been told that self-love is selfish or self-centered or perhaps even narcissistic. It's none of the above. Cultivating self-worth is a pursuit that allows you to enjoy life more fully and deepens your capacity to show love to others, and yourself. When you learn to love yourself, you become better able to love someone else. Research has shown without self-worth we're more likely to get involved in unhealthy relationships, sabotage ourselves when things are going well (we subconsciously don't believe we're worthy) or become dependent on our partner or feel our partner validates us. All these behaviors are self-destructive and move us away from leading an authentic life. I think it's fair to say that you can only experience the depth of love and connection that you ultimately feel for yourself.

So, this book is not just a feel-good roadmap to finding love–a speak positive mantras book–although words have immense power–it's about really digging deep and discovering and defining our true selves. ***It's a journey to self-worth.*** This book primarily focuses on developing healthy relationships, with yourself, friends, family, and potentially a significant other. But we'll also touch on the guiding light of self-worth in other areas of your life, like realizing your calling and passion through business. Many female entrepreneurs either don't pursue or fall short of realizing their true potential because of self-limiting beliefs. We don't live a passion-focused life because we don't feel "we should"' or "could." But going back to relationships. How many times have you "settled" when dating or selecting a partner. Perhaps he didn't check all the boxes for your ideal man, but you've been told by friends and perhaps family that your standards are too high, and after all he does possess some nice qualities. Over time, you heard yourself saying things like, "Not everyone is perfect," "Most of the good men are taken," or "Men in my age bracket are only interested in younger women, so this guy is fine."

If you've ever said these statements to yourself or when confiding in a friend, I'm so glad you're here. These false narratives are little more than shade for your fears. The fear of being disappointed, the fear of being hurt or betrayed. It's time to move beyond this limiting self-talk *and* to move beyond living in the past. The goal is to build a strong foundation on which your dreams and aspirations reside and flourish.

The truth is when we invest time and effort into our personal growth, we become more self-aware, confident, empowered, and emotionally resilient. These qualities not only enhance our own well-being but also positively impact our relationships *and* our choices. We step up to becoming a better version of ourselves, which attracts men of similar qualities. Men, like women, want to feel appreciated for who they are not judged or held accountable for past trespasses they didn't commit. In the following pages, we'll explore how to take things from your past that serve you and leave behind what does not. Our past does not define our future unless we allow it to do so.

As women, we represent so many different roles. Whether it's partner, mother, grandparent, friend, daughter, career woman, sister, to name but a few. Women are often the anchor in a family. People rely on us. But over time, we may forget or confuse our identity . . . who we truly are. I've spoken with so many women who feel they've lost touch with a part of themselves. Years of defining their lives through the lens of others has compromised their sense of self-worth.

Rediscovering your true self is a wonderful path to reconnecting with your life purpose, to understand your core values, and live life on your terms with people, including a new life partner, one who complements *your* authenticity.

So, let's strive to age upwards. An empowering term that means we embrace the beauty of who we are and who we are becoming. It means defining a framework of self-worth and resetting expectations for the life you want moving forward. To live consciously based on what is healthy and fulfilling for you—mind, body, *and* soul.

This book has been written to make you think, reflect, and reassess. To embrace and let go. To explore your dreams and desires. To feel empowered and confident when writing the script for your next chapter. Your path to self-worth involves several important steps. It may seem like a lot, but each step builds on the others.

Following your heart is a journey, and it may require both courage and perseverance. Trust yourself, be patient, and embrace the growth and transformation that comes from aligning your life with your self-worth.

CHAPTER TWO

GUIDED BY PURPOSE

Discovering Your North Star and Life Alignment

*It's all about falling in love with yourself
and sharing that love with someone who appreciates you,
rather than looking for love to compensate
for a self-love deficit.*

\- EARTHA KITT

OVER FIFTY, CONGRATULATIONS! ON THE PATH TO FIFTY, WELCOME TO THE CLUB!

Many research studies, including an expansive study conducted by **Stanford University**[3], shows that not only are we living longer, but that we're happier as we age and more emotionally stable. Many life pressures fall to the side as we mature. Family responsibilities and career pursuits that filled our time and assumed our attention lessen or are redefined.

With longer lifespans, increased happiness and emotional stability, and fewer day-to-day distractions, this may be *the* best stage of life to pursue love again. So, let's start the journey.

HOW WELL DO YOU REALLY KNOW YOURSELF?

The word authenticity is commonly defined as, "living your life according to your own values and goals, rather than those of other people." Put simply, authenticity means you're true to your own personality, values, and spirit, regardless of the pressure that you're under to act otherwise. Too often, we live in fear of other people's opinions or FOPO. We compare ourselves to others and allow outside opinions to guide our behavior. As you might imagine, this hurts our self-esteem. In chapter one, I mentioned that self-confidence can be transient. You can feel on top of the world one moment and feel absolutely crushed the next. This emotional roller coaster can be exhausting. Learning to appreciate and take advantage of your best traits and personal values leads to true happiness rather than the fleeting gratification that comes when someone extends their approval.

Being true to ourselves starts with understanding. The path to self-reflection and awareness can be humbling, fun, unsettling, yet transformative. Nobody is judging you on this journey of personal development. Honesty is key. To get to where you want to go, you must first know where you are.

Every so often, we should take inventory of the things in our life that don't serve us– whether it's negative thinking, focusing on personal flaws (we are often our harshest critics), or unhealthy relationships … past and present. The best way to judge what to let go is to understand who you are and what matters to you most.

Understanding your core principals is foundational, super important, key (I'm trying to make an emphatic point) to uncovering your authentic self. The principles you value will determine how you live your life. They're the standards that you establish for yourself. *Simply stated, principles are the fundamental truths that serve as the foundation for a belief or behavior.* Establishing a set of principles creates a compass to which you can refer whenever something is in doubt, or you need to take a stand, or evaluate a particular opportunity, behavior, or situation. *Principles should drive your values and goals.*

Although we often use the terms values and beliefs interchangeably, they are distinctly different. Values are important when expressing your individual beliefs and opinions. Values are your guiding compass that follow your principles. Beliefs are your assumptions about the world based on your life experiences. Beliefs are a strong emotional state of certainty that you hold about a specific thing, people, or experience in life. Sometimes it's the sense that something simply "feels right."

You'll find that every decision you make is controlled by your beliefs *and* values. Limiting beliefs influence what you focus on and the decisions you make. *What do you want your life to look like?* If you're reading this book, part of your vision likely includes a healthy and loving relationship. We must first look at the lens through which we see the world. As our lens shapes *how* we interpret the world. Our emotional state influences everything. Do you believe that things happen to you or for you? Where we live emotionally impacts our decisions, and our decisions are our destiny. Many times, we simply don't think about where "we live" emotionally. We may think we are eternal optimists, but I'd encourage you to challenge your assumptions and take time to reflect.

Understanding your existing beliefs and reshaping negative beliefs into those that empower you is an important step to *creating* your life. The word "creating" is deliberately chosen in this context to mean progress. **It means we have a choice and can design our future.** We often go through life unconsciously reacting to things and people based on our chosen interpretation of events. When you go down this path further, you'll likely find that some of the stories you've told yourself many times over the years are absolute nonsense. Empowerment stems from our ability to respond, to rewrite the narratives and the stories we've told ourselves. To start living from the inside out rather than the outside in. Although we'll explore this concept in greater detail in a future chapter, living outside-in is typically seen in people who feel victimized. Rather than assuming responsibility for their lives, they focus on the weaknesses of other people or external circumstances as an excuse for who they are and where they are in life. Living inside-out is when your principles guide your behavior. It's liberating to realize your strengths *and* weaknesses.

Your principles and values should stand on their own merit, not be swayed by negative beliefs that don't serve you. Our lives are a series of choices. Every decision, thought, and action defines your destiny. This reality can be humbling if you don't like where you are right now but empowering if you consider that you can learn from the past, embrace the present, and define your future. Taking one step forward leads to multiple steps and then to an entire journey: Our life. This concept is eloquently captured by Billy Graham in the following quote:

> *"It is your decisions, and not your circumstance, that determines your destiny. The strongest principle of life and blessings lies in our choice. Our life is the sum result of all the choices we make, both consciously and unconsciously."*

So, take a breath and ask yourself, *What are my principles?* Some of the most common and widely considered principals include integrity, accountability, fidelity, diligence, compassion, contribution, perseverance, and discipline. Reflect on what truly matters to you. What do you stand for? By aligning your core values, actions, and choices with your principles, you can live a more authentic and fulfilling life.

Take a few moments and review the following worksheets. List your core principles recognizing that they may have changed over time. What you held dear in your twenties or even thirties is likely to be different at this stage of your life. After you've written your list, crystalize them in your mind by adding a short statement about what each means to you. These should be concise and written in your own words. For example, a core principle of mine is integrity. The value I place on this core principle of integrity is defined simply as know and do what is right, always. Give yourself this gift of investing time to go through this exercise.

YOUR NORTH STAR

Before you start on your list, I'd like to encourage you to be still. Be mindful and think about your principles and values.

Creating mental space for reflection will allow you to delve deeper into your thoughts, emotions, and experiences. It may sound silly to some, perhaps a bit "out there" for others, but what I've come to realize is that we don't know our true selves very well. We just go through the motions of life. Mindfulness or meditation helps us to gain clarity.

Journaling is a more tactical form of mindfulness. When journaling, one thing to note is that your journal is <u>your</u> private space, not one to be shared. This comfort of privacy will hopefully give you license to write whatever you feel without judgement. Sometimes, I start by writing what comes to mind whether it's on topic or just random streaming consciousness. Getting below the noise is where the magic happens. It's where we start to hear the whispering of our hearts. There have been days when I simply write, "I don't know what to say," on multiple pages. It's like a mental block that I can't push through. The next day, I start to mentally ramble and realize there's gold beneath my mental noise. I reflect on things that have happened or ideas that I've pondered and slowly moments of insight and brilliance emerge (brilliance may be a bit of an exaggeration, but amazing ideas may surface from a guided mind).

So, the goal of our first exercise together is for you to try meditation and journal what matters most to you. What principles do you covet? This is not a list of "want to haves" for the man of your dreams. **This is about understanding the beauty of who you are.**

Either in your journal or by following the outline below, give yourself the gift of completing the following steps:

- *WRITE* - The principles that are important to you and those that guide your actions and decisions. Write down as many as come to mind, without judgment or limitation. Then, add a short and concise statement about what each principle means to you. Why is it important and where has each principle been demonstrated in your life? How have they served you?

- ***REFLECT -*** Take time to reflect and identify moments when you felt fulfilled, proud, or aligned with your values. Consider situations where you made choices that were in sync with your principles and values and how those choices positively impacted your life.

- ***REVIEW –*** When we take the time to write things down, it's easier for us to see our patterns or the recurring themes that have influenced our lives. Notice if certain values consistently emerge as important contributors to your happiness, growth, and sense of fulfillment. Pay particular attention to the values that have guided your decisions and actions.

- ***PRIORITIZE –*** Now that you have your list, review your values and prioritize them based on their importance to you. For example, consider which values are non-negotiable and fundamental to your sense of self. Rank them in order of importance with the most important values at the top of your list.

YOUR NORTH STAR

YOUR PRINCIPLES	WHY ARE THEY IMPORTANT TO YOU?	RATE THEIR IMPORTANCE

TAKE TIME TO REFLECT

MY VALUES & PERSONAL EXPERIENCES

As you went through this exercise, I hope you gained clarity on what you stand for–your North Star. If it wasn't crystal clear this time, it will come. Through reflection and writing you should start to recognize the guiding principles that have shaped your decisions and actions, leading to a deeper understanding of who you are and what truly matters to you.

Your principles and personal values will and should influence your relationships, present and future. When seeking a life partner, someone with whom you can share a healthy and loving relationship, you want to consciously seek someone who is aligned with your values and some-one who shares your beliefs. It's this strong foundation that encourages ongoing growth. It's easier to become each other's advocate and cheer-leader rather than competitor, each trying to convince the other that their belief system and values are more important. When I reflect on my relationships, I realize the ease that came from an alignment with my North Star and the struggles and heartaches that I felt when the alignment didn't exist.

Stephen Covey, in his acclaimed book, *The 7 Habits of Highly Effective People*[4], refers to aligning one's values with universal and timeless principles as the Character Ethic. It's the wisdom to guide your actions based on what is most important to you, your values. If we defer to external influences and opinions to guide us, we can lose ourselves. Our principles should be our North Star, our internal compass. Which is why it's important to go through this first exercise to put a personal spotlight on your principles and values and to appreciate why they're important to you.

> *"Until you make the unconscious conscious, it will*
> *direct your life and you will call it fate."*
> - C.G. Jung

LET'S CELEBRATE OUR UNIQUENESS!

It's the beautiful tapestry of life. Recognizing your unique strengths, abilities and talents can help you gain an even deeper appreciation of who you are as an individual. This can be a wonderful catalyst for personal growth and the start of your journey to discover what really moves you. By embracing and celebrating your strengths, you cultivate self-worth and a belief in yourself, which encourages you to live more authentically and ultimately enjoy a greater sense of happiness and fulfillment.

There have been times in my life, perhaps you can relate, when I compromised myself on behalf of the man I was married to or in a relationship with. I was drawn to powerful men who were highly credentialed and accomplished. None of which is bad. What was self-limiting was my belief that my abilities and natural talents were not enough. I downplayed or understated the value of my strengths, due to self-doubt and social expectations. The fact that I'm a "creative" at heart is something I stifled … after all, I should be an accomplished businesswoman climbing the corporate ladder of success … no matter the personal cost. This impacted not only my relationships, but the level of success I *allowed* myself to achieve.

I finally realized that celebrating my strengths was transformative as it empowered me to live a life of authenticity, confidence, and purpose. But for those of you who have bravely ventured down this path, I'm sure many have hit the "imposter syndrome" wall. We've convinced ourselves for so long that our strengths may not live up to other people's expectations or they're not all that important, so we second guess ourselves and sabotage our efforts to change. Our primitive brains, that part of our mind that is squarely focused on keeping us safe, joins the parade and we stay stuck. It was a nice thought, but unrealistic and fanciful after all.

But just imagine unlocking your full potential and relishing in the positive impact it has on your life and the lives of those around you. Following your natural passions in alignment with your values will enhance how you live and foster a natural momentum forward. Living life authentically, aligned to your passions, will give you a unique aura of contentment–one that is contagious. You may be surprised at the impact you can have on other people–perhaps you become their role model or source of inspiration. What a wonderful gift to give to yourself *and* others!

Let's have some fun. Think about a time when you felt light, free, and completely content. When laughter flowed, everything seemed to fall into place and time stood still. What were you doing? This feeling of oneness is what living in harmony with your inner self, strengths, and talents feels like.

I love to sculpt. The tactile nature of creating something or someone out of a block of clay is soulful for me. Am I going to be a professional sculptor? No. But immersing myself in this expression helps me to stay connected. My mind stops, and I just lose myself in simply being present. It feeds my soul. I encourage you, if you haven't already done so, to find something that is soulful for you. For some people it's gardening or being one with nature. Whatever it may be, seek to find something that really moves you, spiritually and soulfully.

Celebrating your strengths in a relationship is not just about acknowledging what you're good at …. although that's pretty cool. It's about understanding how your unique abilities can contribute to a healthier, more balanced, and fulfilling relationship. Let's lean into some ways this is beneficial.

When you acknowledge and demonstrate your strengths, it fosters a sense of mutual respect in a relationship. You give your partner a window into your soul and an opportunity to admire your abilities and appreciate the unique qualities you bring to the table. Equally important is that mutual respect promotes a sense of emotional security and accountability in a partnership and encourages more open communication. If you believe your unique strengths and talents are appreciated and valued you feel more secure. Security can create a safe place for personal expression rather than a feeling of hiding in plain sight.

SHARE YOUR ACHIEVEMENTS

Don't shy away from sharing your achievements with others. It's not boastful but rather a gift to *allow* people who love you to share in your success. Early in our relationship, Mark and I were boating when I received notification that a photograph I had submitted to a gallery won Best in Show. Mark seemed as excited as I felt. He quickly stopped the boat in the middle of the Chesapeake Bay so we could have a champagne toast to my success. His support and excitement made this accomplishment even more special.

SET PERSONAL PASSION GOALS (NOT ANOTHER DREADED TO-DO LIST)

Is there something you've always want to do but have been putting off? Something soulful. Perhaps writing a book, playing pickleball, taking up photography or painting. Whatever pursuit you feel passionate about will foster greater excitement in your life … trust me! Excitement about personal passions will inspire you to realize your goals, which will build your self-confidence and self-worth, which will help you to achieve more things that you enjoy and help you to navigate finding and sharing healthy love again. There's a beautiful colored ribbon that connects all these dots in our life.

The powerful impact of living with passion and being aligned with what inspires you cannot be overstated. *Fulfilling your life passions through a vision of inspiration fostered by meaningful change—now that's a worthy goal.* So where to begin?

START WITH THE END IN MIND

Rather than simply going through life and then wondering where the last three or perhaps even ten years went, let's design this next chapter. If you've ever seen the *Christmas Carol* by Charles Dickens, you may recall the ghosts that appeared to Ebenezer Scrooge. They illuminated what his future life would be like if he did nothing to change. If we strive for something different, perhaps something better or more fulfilling, it's up to us to bring it to light. We *can* create the life we want rather than the life other people dictate. Integrating your passions with your life goals will help you to realize greater balance. A healthier life balance will feed your soul and inspire your passion. So, ask yourself, *If not now, when?*

IT'S TIME TO PRIORITIZE YOUR OWN NEEDS

I hear many women say they're content, but when pushed they realize they've simply settled. Consider this time to be the last chapter of your life … a long chapter we all hope. I don't know about you, but I want to live it with unbridled enthusiasm. It was the *Christmas Carol* exercise demonstrated during a Tony Robbins seminar that was my wake-up call. I was "content," but the vision of having nothing in my life change five or ten years down the road brought me to tears. I was sobbing. This reaction really startled me. I wasn't unhappy, but in my heart, I wanted more. I felt I deserved more out of my life. It was then I decided to invest in myself so *I could create my path forward*. What do you want from your next chapter? This is something to ponder. Really think about this question and be specific about what it is that you want and why. We all need a purpose and reason to change. Going back to our primitive brains, we are controlled by fear and pleasure. If the fear of change is not replaced with the pleasure of making that change nothing will change. For example, simply saying you need to lose weight is not enough. You may lose a few pounds, but if the pleasure of eating is stronger than the pleasure of being slimmer, you'll likely put the pounds back on. We need to relish in the pleasure of enjoying a healthier body and living life with more energy. That's a motivator for sustained behavior change … it replaces the pleasure of eating and puts the focus on the benefit of the result.

When you are passionate about something, you naturally feel more energized, focused, and determined to achieve it. Passion fuels our commitment and perseverance, helping us to overcome obstacles and stay dedicated to our goals, even in the face of challenges. The opposite holds true when we betray ourselves. Unlike when I sculpt and the hours seem like minutes, doing something that contradicts what really speaks to me and feeds my soul is like taking air out of the room. I struggle to exist through the moments that seem like hours.

We are all holistic beings that thrive when living in harmony. Personal passion goals are rooted in your authentic desires and interests. When you set goals aligned with your passions, you create a pathway (perhaps even an expressway) towards personal fulfillment and a sense of purpose. Pursuing what you are genuinely passionate about brings joy, satisfaction, and a deep sense of meaning to your life. It's a connection with your inner self.

What is also interesting to experience is the confidence we develop when we're living authentically. It's like a key that unlocks the self-assurance we need to step outside of our comfort zones. This confidence encourages personal growth and development, which leads to, you guessed it, self-worth. This book exists because I had a wake-up call that led me down a path of personal growth that led me to the life I cherish today. This is not a dress rehearsal. When I was a young girl, I remember an older woman saying that time speeds up as we age. We get only one shot. I decided it was no longer acceptable for me to make excuses another year or two or more. This time, I promised myself I would honor the woman I am. I encourage you to do the same.

We've talked a lot about authenticity. What is the value of authenticity in a relationship? *It's how we should show up.* When both partners embrace their unique set of strengths and pursue their passions, there's a natural balance or complement that is introduced. Sharing your strengths creates an environment where you can be supportive of each other's setbacks and celebrate your successes! It helps to create an open and safe environment where you feel inclined to explore your strengths more fully knowing that they're appreciated by both you *and* your partner. It's a relationship where you can try and fail and try again, knowing that you are with someone who has your back. A healthy relationship that is founded on principles and defined by self-worth gives you space to be accepted simply for who you are today and who you are striving to become tomorrow.

Before I continue talking about the importance of celebrating our strengths, we all know we have weaknesses. Embracing your strengths doesn't mean you ignore your weaknesses. But let's be honest, we're all flawed. It's unrealistic to think we are ever going to reach perfection … it's simply unattainable. Our path to personal development puts a spotlight on our strengths. By understanding your strengths, you can better identify areas for improvement and work towards becoming a better version of yourself and a better life partner. But we always need to remember that "every great journey starts with a single step." Clarity about our strengths and areas for improvement tends to make us less defensive. We recognize we're not perfect. We celebrate and cultivate our strengths. And we determine what areas of improvement need our attention. This can lead to a deeper understanding and stronger connection between you and your partner. People who live in glass houses can be difficult to be around. Developing a strong sense of emotional intelligence about ourselves makes it easier to grow and easier for people to support our growth and share our lives.

Let's take a few moments so you can think about your unique strengths and think about how they have and can serve you. It's interesting that many women I've spoken with have a hard time with this exercise. They struggle to place value on an extensive list of their strengths and what they do write down is more about what they do for others. I encourage you to simply start writing whether it's on the following pages or in your journal. Don't judge yourself and just allow your pen or pencil to get below the mental noise.

REFLECT ON YOUR STRENGTHS

Try to think openly and without judgement. Your strengths may vary in terms of what you perceive to be significant, but they're *your* unique strengths. Start with writing your list of unique strengths on the left. In the right column, reflect on how your strengths have contributed to your achievements and happiness in life. This should be a fun exercise, one that can help you appreciate your unique qualities and talents.

MY STRENGTHS	HOW HAVE THEY SERVED ME?

BECOME YOUR BEST CHEERLEADER

There are so many reasons why acknowledging your uniqueness is important. To start, it validates your self-worth, accomplishments, and strengths. It's about giving yourself credit for your efforts and achievements, no matter how big or small. It helps to boost your self-confidence when you acknowledge your capabilities and believe in your potential. And it fosters self-compassion, which can help you to become your best cheerleader, so you treat yourself with kindness, compassion, and understanding. It fosters grace to accept mistakes as part of your journey. By accepting yourself and honoring your uniqueness you feel more empowered to show up fully and authentically in your relationships and life in general, and you feel more confident in celebrating the amazing woman you have become, not perfect but amazing, nonetheless.

The natural beauty that surrounds us never ceases to amaze and humble me. Although synergy and balance abound, so, too, does imperfection. Sometimes, it's the imperfections in life that are the most beautiful. I love going to art shows and often see a wood sculptor who creates the most amazing decorative pieces. Part of the magnificence of these pieces is the wood burl. It's not perfectly symmetrical or perfect at all, which enhances the natural beauty of each piece.

For those of us who strive to overachieve, remember personal growth doesn't happen overnight. It's a process. Although patience may not be one of your strengths, I would ask that you give yourself this grace. The amazing thing about change is that it comes with a new set of lenses through which you see new levels of growth you may never have believed yourself capable of seeing. Soon, you'll need a telescope to see where you started.

THE POWER OF GRATITUDE

In earlier pages, I shared the multiple benefits of journaling and meditation. Another practice that can influence how you view life and how you view yourself is gratitude. It's so easy to change our state of mind or have it changed for us. Taking conscious steps to *controlling* how we experience life will influence how your life unfolds. A quick story. At the start of my career, I worked with a woman who proudly displayed in her cubicle (that dates me, I'm sure) a sign that said, *Life sucks and then you die.* I remember being absolutely appalled but realized her misery to a great extent was self-inflicted. We all have a choice as to how we interpret life. Gratitude is one of our superpowers. It guides us to seek the positive in every situation, which then allows us to enjoy life more fully, which means we send out positive vibes, which attracts more positive situations and people. If you're skeptical, give it a try.

Here's a simple way to begin. Today, we've all become so reliant on our technical devices. Are you one of the many who reaches for their phone first thing in this morning, whether to read texts, emails, get the latest scoop on your favorite social media platform, or perhaps catch up on what's going on in the world? If your answer is "yes", I encourage you to try something different tomorrow. Start your day with gratitude and experience the difference in how you feel. Lie in bed or sit cross-legged on the floor, whatever makes you most comfortable, and simply think about your blessings. Starting your day with gratitude gives *you* the power to control your emotional state from the inside out rather than letting external things and people influence how you feel. For those of you who are in marketing, you understand the intentional emotional tug of advertisements and headlines. Sensationalism sells. It's how businesses drive revenue. I encourage you to not allow this external pull to define how you start each day. Expressing gratitude can brighten your outlook, boost your mood, and help you feel more positive in the face of challenges . . . a much healthier and empowering start.

Each morning, I spend a few minutes expressing gratitude for myself, for those I love, and for the things in my life for which I'm most grateful. The order is important as praising your gifts and strengths first helps to create a more positive lens through which you look at your life. This may be difficult for some of you as you're so programmed to think poorly of yourself. But this morning ritual can help you to appreciate the woman you are, and the woman you're becoming. Gratitude has been heralded throughout history as the *mother of all virtues* given its impact. It changes our physiology and helps us to feel more positive—the empowerment that will support your growth is within you.

Another fun exercise in self-reflection involves listing your blessings. My hope is that you'll be pleasantly surprised about how many things for which you can be grateful exist in your life–big and small. But sometimes, we all feel overwhelmed or that we're fighting against the tide. Contemplate every detail of your life, big and small, and just start writing. I'm repeating myself I know, but when we write things down it allows our minds to get below the noise. The stories we tell ourselves can be ingrained, but eventually we get to the essence of what is most important. The things we're grateful for.

| I"M GRATEFUL FOR . . . I LOVE MY LIFE BECAUSE . . . |

Before we leave this chapter, list some personal passion goals, things you may be doing and things you want to be doing. A goal that is not written down is nothing more than a wish. So, take some time to write down those passion goals you want to become a reality. You may want to meditate first to clear your mind and gain clarity. It's too easy to simply go through the motions of life without truly living our passions. Once listed, rate your conviction to achieve these goals. Then, write a date next to those with the highest rating. Create a vision for yourself about living your life with more passion. Remember, you deserve more!

MY PERSONAL PASSION GOALS	MY CONVICTION LEVEL Scale 1-10	MY "BY WHEN" COMMITMENT

This chapter was written to help you lay the foundation for what's next. We covered how to embrace your authentic self and went through an exercise that illuminated your core values and recognized the influence they've had on your life. You celebrated your unique qualities and strengths and learned the power and value of gratitude, of appreciating the small and large blessings that make up your life.

Now let's move on to honoring your past: After all, it's helped to shape the beautiful woman you've become. The goal of the next chapter is to gain clarity about how your past has influenced your beliefs and then learn that you have the power to rewrite some of the stories that may have held you back. You can't change historical events, but you can change your belief about their purpose and impact. And you can change how you decide to write your stories.

CHAPTER THREE

LEGACY OF RESILIENCE

Embracing Past Lessons for a Brighter Future

*"Your wounds are the sacred temple
in which you have been transformed."*

- DR. BARBARA DEANGELIS

’ll be the first to acknowledge that it took me a while to forgive my ex-husband and to assume shared responsibility for what happened. Unless there’s an extreme situation, I think it’s fair to say we’re all part of both the problem *and* solution. Learning to take valuable lessons from each experience and insights that become wisdom to serve you as you pursue love again is the goal of this chapter.

A quick story. A friend of mine, we’ll call her Julie, is beautiful, energetic, fun, smart, and yet she’s damaged. Men are easily attracted to her looks and positive energy. She so wants to share a healthy relationship, but she’s not emotionally whole. There’s a part of her that fears getting hurt again. Her emotional conflict continues to subconsciously sabotage her efforts. As her relationships become more intense, her barriers go up. She pushes men away to prevent herself from being hurt more deeply as if every man is a clone of her ex-husband. Perhaps you can relate. If so, you’re not alone.

It’s easy to stack fear, which then leads to our emotional barriers. We set ourselves up to relive the same painful experience, which reinforces the reason for our fears. The emotional stacking continues, and the barriers become more entrenched.

If, like Julie, the past is holding you back then letting go is a *must* so you can move forward. To harbor resentment or anger only hurts you.[5]

The five years I spent dealing with Graves’ Disease was terrible. But I gained tremendous strength and resilience from fighting my way to the other side. I realized my true value below the surface persona of simply being a “pretty face”, which is how I felt when I was modeling. This life experience is one that I’ve learned to embrace as part of my journey to where I am today. It’s given me the inner resolve to persevere and to never take my health for granted. It was a gift, one opened perhaps later in life, but a true gift, nonetheless. There is a healthy approach to reflection through which you can gain perspective. Often, some of your past hurts and disappointments were your greatest times of personal growth. It’s all a matter of changing the way you look at your past. To *rewrite the meaning of your personal stories.*

Before we move forward, I'd like to encourage you to think about the questions you ask yourself. I heard this concept from Tony Robbins. The more I considered this view the more of an "aha" moment I experienced. Our minds are incredibly powerful, and they can find or create answers to just about any question we ask ourselves. So, we need to really pay attention to those questions. Let's use an example. If you ask yourself questions like, *Why does this always happen to me?* or *Why do I always meet losers?* or *How come my life isn't where it should be?* your mind will kindly delivery a variety of self-deflating answers. Our minds are geared to finding answers to the questions we consistently ask ourselves. Questions are the basis for every decision we make. *So, let's ask ourselves better questions.* It sounds so simple, but unless we think about it consciously, it's likely we'll ask the same questions that continue to undermine our happiness. Rather than asking the *why* questions try switching to *what* or *how.* For example, rather than asking, *Why does this always happen to me?* when a situation repeats, try asking, *What can I learn from this, so I can create a better outcome for myself?* It may seem like a subtle shift, but the answers you'll present in your mind will be empowering rather than deflating. The more you ask yourself questions that align to *What can I learn?* or *How can I benefit or embrace this to help me move forward?* the more your mind will focus on the positives rather than getting stuck in the endless loop of negative thoughts. As you go through the process of reflecting on your past, consider the questions that come into your mind. *Be conscious about asking questions that will empower you to find the positive outcomes and answers that will serve you.*

Moving forward and uncovering the lessons and wisdoms from your past can be guided by a thoughtful and introspective process that includes *reflection, gratitude, self-compassion, release and letting go, extracting wisdom, and then integrating that wisdom into your new stories.* Let's explore each of these areas, as honoring your past is not only about pulling forth insights and learnings but helping to release yourself from your past. You will find that these steps are laid out in a logical sequence to guide you through the process.

Reflecting on past experiences, including those that may have been difficult or hurtful, can be challenging but an important part of personal growth. Find a quiet and comfortable environment where you can reflect without distractions … anywhere you feel at ease. One of my favorite places is the beach at dusk. The colors remind me of a watercolor painting and the sounds are so rhythmic that I feel completely relaxed and at peace. Go to wherever speaks to *your*heart with journal in hand, so can write down your thoughts and feelings. Start by describing the specific experience or event that was difficult or hurtful. Allow yourself to express your emotions and thoughts freely.

Relax and tune into your emotions and try to acknowledge them without judgment. This can be hard if you're still angry with someone who hurt you, but it *doesn't help you to place blame* … this is *your* healing journey. Allow yourself to feel whatever comes up, whether it's sadness, anger, or frustration. Give yourself permission to experience a range of emotions during your reflective moments.

When I was dealing with my divorce and the likely disappointment of not having children, I went through this exercise. My wedding was magical (although most brides would likely say the same thing). The ceremony and reception were held outdoors at a beautiful venue in Northern Virginia—The Oatlands Plantation.

A few months after our divorce, I decided to go back early one Sunday. I relived our wedding by walking the grounds remembering every moment in my mind, thinking about the promise I felt about my future. Emotionally exhausted, I finally sat down at the reflecting pool where the wedding toast was made and simply cried. With my journal in hand, I scribbled down everything I felt and the hard lessons I learned. It was humbling to realize the wheel of circumstances that led me down that path, so I pledged to learn from this mistake … which I did, but at the time, I was less focused on my personal growth. My takeaway at the time was focused more about paying attention to "red flags." The illumination that I needed to change and grow personally came later. I hope you embrace the opportunity to shorten your time to greater fulfillment.

Although this may be difficult, try to gain a broader perspective on the situations that come to mind. Consider the factors that may have contributed to your difficulty or hurt, including your own actions, the actions of others, and any external circumstances. This can help you to understand the situation from different angles rather than simply finding fault.

Honestly think about what you learned. What lessons or insights can you take from your past experiences? Reflect on how the experience has shaped you and look for the positive changes it has brought about.

If the experience you're reflecting on is particularly difficult or traumatic, consider seeking support from a trusted friend, family member, or even a therapist. They can provide guidance, empathy, and a safe space for you to process your emotions.

Reflecting and honoring your past is a process. It's okay if you don't have all the answers right away, and it's okay if you only focus on one thing at a time. Be patient with yourself and allow the process to unfold naturally. By reflecting on difficult experiences, you can gain valuable insights that help to pave the way for healing and personal growth. This process may prove to be both positive and challenging, but the takeaways will include cultivating more confidence about how your past can and has served you.

Sister Shivani, a well-respected spiritual guide, speaks in-depth about the importance of letting go of pain, anger, or an unwillingness to forgive. *Happiness equals emotional independence, it's our power.* When you forgive someone, you're really forgiving yourself as you're the only person you can forgive. It won't change the consequences of Karma. But every time we share or relive a hurtful experience or event it's like scratching the same wound. Don't look at your past with fear and allow someone from your past to spoil your life. Your mind is your greatest gift. Train it to serve you. Ask the right questions.

Stive to express *gratitude* for the lessons and experiences that have shaped you. Acknowledge the value they have brought to your life and the opportunities for growth they have provided. Practicing gratitude when honoring your past can involve:

- *Recognizing* the people who supported you
- *Appreciating* the lessons and personal growth you realized
- *Being grateful* for the skills and knowledge you gained
- *Acknowledging* the opportunities that arose as a result. The adage *when one door closes another door opens* is so true

I was raised in a wonderful English family. My parents kept their emotions close to their chest and I learned to do the same. One of the hardest moments for me with Graves' Disease was that I looked sick. Honestly, I looked terrible. It would have been easier for me if I could have fought this illness in private, but I couldn't. The signs were overly visible. The blessing of this humbling experience was that I learned to let people into my world. A world that felt as if it were crumbling around me at the time. I learned to rely on people, to share my innermost fears. This life experience helped me to grow and helped me to openly share myself with others. This is a gift for which I am so grateful.

I'm sure you can think of many occasions during your life when you experienced this gift. Our challenge is to not be blinded by our past. Otherwise, we are not open to seeing new doors let alone be able to walk through them.

By cultivating a mindset of gratitude, you shift your focus to the positive aspects of your past experiences, which can help you to maintain a positive outlook and attract more positive experiences in the future. Gratitude is a practiced art, so you may catch yourself defaulting to negative narratives. Perseverance is what will result in change. Asking questions that allow you to find the grace and gift of growth is an important step in your journey.

SELF-COMPASSION

Expressing self-compassion when reflecting and learning from your past is essential. Here are some things to consider during this process.

Try to be present and aware of your thoughts and emotions as you reflect. Notice any self-critical or judgmental thoughts that arise. Instead of getting caught up in them, gently redirect your attention to a place of understanding and self-compassion.

Enlist your kind and supportive inner voice. A compassionate inner voice is beneficial in all areas of your life, but even more important when reflecting on past experiences that may be difficult or disappointing. Think about how you would treat a friend who is going through a difficult time and offer yourself words of encouragement, comfort, and reassurance.

Recognize that everyone makes mistakes and faces challenges. Embrace your imperfections and realize that you're simply human and not alone—we're all flawed. Instead of dwelling on perceived failures, focus on the lessons learned and the growth that has come from your experiences.

Forgive yourself for any mistakes or regrets from the past. It's always unfair to judge ourselves in retrospect. As the saying goes, *hindsight is 20/20.* Understand that you were doing the best you could with the knowledge and resources you had at that time. Release self-blame or guilt and allow yourself to move forward with a sense of forgiveness and compassion.

You will likely feel a variety of emotions as you walk through this process whether sadness, anger, or regret. Give yourself permission to feel these emotions and offer yourself comfort and understanding so you can release those emotions that have tied you to the past.

Celebrate the wisdom and strength you have gained from your past experiences to help anchor appreciation and a positive focus.

Our vulnerability is often exposed when we reconsider our past. Treat yourself with kindness, understanding, and love as you reflect on how you grew from your past experiences. In the next chapter we will delve more deeply into ways you can cultivate deeper self-love and self-worth.

RELEASE AND LET GO

Ask yourself, *What am I holding onto that doesn't serve me?* Emotional barriers can include regrets, resentments, grudges, or any negative emotions that are weighing you down. These emotions can become your proverbial ball and chain. It's easy for us to hold onto emotions that have become our stories. We create stories, interpretations of life events, to explain or justify why things happened to us. But we don't do ourselves any favors by holding onto to disempowering emotions. I've spoken with many women who almost celebrate the walls they've built over time. They present these walls as a challenge to any future man that ventures into their lives. Our protective walls only hinder our progress and prevent us from fully embracing the present, and future. Getting to the source and navigating through our walls is where healing and empowerment is realized. A wake-up call for us all is the realization that the people about whom we harbor resentment or anger have more than likely moved on—we're the ones still being hurt. We shouldn't give away our power to choose a happier future.

As William Shakespeare so divinely stated in his play, *The Tempest*, "If past is prologue." By honestly acknowledging what happened in our past, the good, the bad, and the ugly, we help craft a path forward. If we continue on autopilot little will likely change. Protective walls may seem like a good way to prevent hurt, but they put us into a reactive mode. Rather than looking for good from a position of self-understanding, we're looking and waiting for inevitable "bad" to happen. Which means we're focusing on the negative, or potential negative, which is even worse. Which brings us to: *Acceptance*

Acknowledge that you cannot change the past, but you have the power to shape your present and future. You have the ability within you to rewrite the stories you've told yourself and others over time. Surrender to the fact that certain things are beyond your control and focus on what you *can* control. As Tony Robbins says, "Divorce your story of limitation and marry the truth that you have unlimited possibility."

Journaling and meditation can be your supportive partners and a healthy way to explore and express your emotions. Reflecting and journaling your thoughts, fears, and regrets will help you to experience and process your emotions and then release those that have hindered you. I've personally gone through this exercise and when written on paper some of my stories seemed so silly, but I gave them enormous power to control how I was navigating through life.

Forgiveness is a natural complement to compassion and a powerful tool for letting go. The divine gift of forgiveness should include not only yourself, but other people involved in your past. Understand that forgiveness is not about condoning actions, but about freeing yourself from the emotional burden and finding peace within. It is a gift you give to *yourself!*

Writing New Stories is your opportunity to challenge and reframe negative or limiting beliefs that have kept you anchored to your past. By replacing limiting beliefs with empowering and positive perspectives, you'll find a lightness that supports your growth and well-being. Always try to remember that *we interpret* the events of our lives through our current lens and then turn them into our stories. We can look at events either positively or negatively. Almost every situation presents the option of choice. When reflecting on your past or moving into the future, how do you want to write your stories? Perhaps this concept seems a little difficult to accept but think about the times when you and a friend went to the same event, met the same people, and yet walked away with completely different sentiments about the occasion. What was different? Was it that your friend simply didn't like the "feel" of the place or that one person that you both met was a little loud, whereas you really liked the décor and found the loud person to be funny? It's a matter of perspective. I'm not saying that you won't hold differing opinions but seeking out the positive is as easy as looking for the negative. The question is which serves your happiness?

Shift your focus to the lessons learned and your opportunities for growth. Being grateful for the wisdom gained, the strength developed, and the opportunities for self-discovery that have emerged can be so powerful, and empowering. We'll delve deeper into this topic of rewriting your stories later in this chapter.

RELEASING AND LETTING GO

This takes time and a healthy dose of self-compassion. Give yourself the grace of patience and trust that you can let go of what no longer serves you, allowing emotional space for new possibilities in your life. When I first went through this exercise about my divorce, I went through a roller coaster of emotions. What I found after this process was a sense of lightness and inner peace. I forgave myself and opened my heart.

We don't always realize the physical toll that not forgiving people and holding onto negative emotions can have on our bodies and lives. A study by Karen Swartz, M.D., director of the Mood Disorders Adult Consultative Clinic at Johns Hopkins University[5] stated that, "Chronic anger puts you in a flight-or-fight mode, which results in numerous changes in heart rate, blood pressure and immune response." Forgiveness is an active process when you make a conscious decision to let go of negative feelings whether the person deserves it or not. Forgiveness is a choice. Karma is out of our control.

Integrating the lessons and wisdom from your past into your present and future is a powerful way to honor your journey and *create* positive change in your life. Think of it this way, when we respond versus simply react, we reclaim our power. Our power of choice, our power to make decisions about what we want and how we choose to respond.

Perhaps there are lessons and bits of wisdom from your past that really stand out to you. Take time to identify the specific insights, values, and strengths that have surfaced. Develop an inner awareness about how these lessons can be applied to your present and future.

By stepping back, you'll be able to reflect and look for patterns or recurring themes from your past. Identify any behaviors, beliefs, or choices that have contributed to positive outcomes and challenges in your life. By doing so, you can begin to recognize the patterns that have served you well and those that you may need to adjust moving forward.

Based on the lessons and wisdom you have gained, start setting clear intentions for how you want to integrate them into your life. Define the values and principles that will guide your actions and decisions moving forward. This is a conscious exercise that may start on these pages but will be something you'll carry forward.

Cultivating mindfulness in your daily life will help you to remain present and aware of your thoughts, emotions, and actions. Notice when old patterns or triggers arise, and consciously choose to respond in a way that serves you. Again, be patient. You may have been reliving negative emotions for some time. It will take time to create a more positive end to your story.

Try to become aware of making choices that align with your values and the lessons learned. Take small steps towards your goals and aspirations, integrating the wisdom you have gained along the way. *Celebrate your progress* and learn from any challenges that arise. The pleasure part of your brain will naturally begin to gravitate to new these new behaviors if you affirm and celebrate them. Our brains are hardwired to avoid pain or seek pleasure. Rather than being tethered to the pain of the past, rewrite your stories so they represent the potential of pleasure now, and in the future.

I would encourage you to view your setbacks as opportunities. Try to embrace the idea that your past experiences have equipped you with the wisdom and strength to overcome obstacles and create a fulfilling future. Use these powerful insights to help make informed decisions, set goals, and take steps towards your desired future.

Be *kind and compassionate* towards yourself throughout this process (this is something that bears repeating as we all tend to beat ourselves up emotionally at times). Embrace that growth is a journey, and it's okay to make mistakes or encounter challenges along the way. Treat yourself with patience, love, and forgiveness. *Make peace with your past.*

REWRITE YOUR STORIES

Transformation begins when you're able to integrate and grow from your past—to view your life through a new lens. Here are some steps to help you rewrite the stories you may have carried in your mind that haven't served you.

Psychology Today[6] states that we form our identity by integrating our life experiences into an internalized, evolving story of ourselves, which gives us a sense of unity and purpose. What's interesting to consider is that when you change the meaning and narrative of your past, you simultaneously change the narrative of your present and future. Think about that for a moment. The facts about your past can't change, but the story you tell yourself about them absolutely can.

As Tony Robbins[7] states, "Change your story, change your life." The driving force in our lives are a result of the stories we've told ourselves. They can influence every thought, feeling, and decision. Unfortunately, we often find ourselves on autopilot.

A story is simply the set of beliefs you have about your life and yourself. Limiting stories often blind us from opportunities. We need to shift our perspective from, "Life is happening *to you,* to life is happening *for you." Give yourself the license to become the choreographer of your life rather than a victim of past circumstances.*

Learning how to challenge and reframe the negative stories or beliefs we hold about ourselves or our experiences can help release us from the past and change the narrative about the present and future. This may be a challenge at first as you likely have repeated these stories many times to yourself and others. I've met so many men and women who have allowed themselves to fall into a mindset of "victimology." I'm not diminishing the impact of certain life experiences, but our power is realized in the process of overcoming what has happened and using those experiences to propel us forward. As Sister Shivani stated, "Happiness equals emotional independence—it's our power." Let's reclaim what we've lost over time.

To start, you need to become aware of the negative narratives or self-limiting beliefs that you hold. These narratives often manifest as self-critical thoughts or statements that undermine your confidence or potential. Think about the things you say to yourself and about yourself and notice when these narratives arise and the impact they have on your mindset. We can negatively influence our mood and self-confidence by simply repeating a well-practiced, self-defeating narrative. Some examples might include: "I'm not good enough." "I'm too old." "Men always disappoint me," or "This is just another example of (you can fill in the blanks)."

Challenge Your Negative Narratives by questioning their validity. Ask yourself if there is concrete evidence to support these beliefs or if they are based on assumptions or past experiences that may no longer be relevant. Often, negative narratives are distorted or exaggerated versions of our reality. Sometimes, it helps to ask yourself better questions. Our thoughts are comprised of a series of questions we constantly ask ourselves. Taking control of these questions can be powerful. For example, rather than asking, *Why does this always happen to me?* change the question to help your mind find a positive solution. Like, *I've experienced this before. What steps can I take to have a better outcome, so I'm happier and more fulfilled?* The first question is self-defeating, whereas the second question is empowering. There's a solution to be found that serves you. *Where focus goes energy flows. What we focus on we feel.* The quality of our lives is defined by where we live emotionally. Giving your mind positive instructions will help you to remain focused on what's possible. Our minds will always find the answer to the questions we ask, so why not ask better questions so that you receive better answers?

Take time to pause and look for alternative perspectives or counterexamples that contradict your negative narratives or stories. Seek out *evidence* that supports a more positive and empowering view of yourself and your experiences. This can involve reflecting on past successes, seeking feedback from others, or finding inspiring stories of individuals who have overcome similar challenges. You may beat yourself up emotionally based on one example, one moment in time, whereas there are many other examples when you've demonstrated strength and insight. Cultivate your self-worth by focusing attention on how you've positively managed different situations and circumstances, and then ask yourself what was different. The more time you invest in rewriting your stories and narratives, the more occasion you give yourself to find and appreciate your value. We're not weaving a fantasy of who you are, but by focusing on positive demonstrations of who you are you will become stronger and better equipped to define life on your terms based on what makes you happy.

CLEAR INTENTIONS

Use your past experiences as a foundation for setting clear intentions for your future. How? By identifying the values, skills, and qualities you want to cultivate. By aligning your actions with your intentions, you can grow and evolve in a more positive direction. Again, this is about being consciously aware and taking control of your emotional state.

I've always loved this quote from Stephen Covey as it bestows that your past is already defined, whereas your future has endless possibilities. Possibilities that you can control.

"The past is finite whereas the future is infinite."

PRIMING YOUR MIND

It's an interesting concept to consider that you can indeed train your mind. If you don't take control, outside influences will do it for you. It's why feeding your mind daily is so important. What's equally important is repetition. Hearing, reading, or learning something one time is not enough to change behaviors and mindset. *Repetition is the mother of skill and mastery.* Replace negative narratives with positive affirmations or empowering statements. Create a list of affirmations that challenge your negative beliefs and reinforce positive qualities or possibilities. By repeating these affirmations regularly, you can rewire your thinking patterns and reinforce a more positive self-image. Negative self-talk weakens you. Positive affirmations spoken repeatedly will help to reframe and strengthen your self-image. If you think you're not enough, you'll behave that way and attract less than what you deserve. If you know you're enough, your mind will seek ways to affirm that belief. It goes back to the statement, *Where focus goes energy flows.* I hope now is the time when you begin to take control and give your mind a path to seeking the positive rather than defaulting to self-deflating repetition.

Be kind and compassionate towards yourself as you work on redefining negative narratives. Understand that these narratives may have developed because of past experiences or external influences. Treat yourself with understanding and forgiveness and remind yourself that you have the power t to rewrite the stories of your past so they can *help* your future. *Nowhere does it state that the past must define your future unless you let it.*

Surround yourself with positive influences, whether it's supportive friends, mentors, or uplifting content. There's an adage that states, *misery likes company.* If friends who have commiserated with you in the past seek to hold you back, you may need to distance yourself. Engage in those activities that inspire and motivate you. By immersing yourself in a positive environment, you can counteract the negative narratives and reinforce a more empowering mindset.

Take small, actionable steps towards challenging and reframing your stories. *Celebrate even the smallest victories* along the way. Each step forward builds momentum and reinforces the new positive foundation you are creating. Every time you dismiss a negative view about yourself, the other stories you wrote through a lens of insecurity or lack of self-confidence will have less power over you.

Give yourself the gift of patience and self-compassion. Like anything new, this is a process which will take time. But by consciously challenging and reframing your negative stories and narratives, you *can* cultivate a more positive and empowering view of yourself and your experiences, leading to personal growth and a greater sense of overall well-being.

One of my favorite sayings is that *we are all works in progress.* -The past has contributed to who you are today, but the long-term impact of your past is your choice. The goal is for you to honor your past experiences, but to do so through a lens of personal growth. Approach this with compassion, patience, and self-care so you can, in time, step into your authenticity and create a foundation for a fulfilling and loving future.

Embrace the journey, stay open to new experiences, and trust in your ability to create a meaningful and fulfilling future based on the wisdom you have gained. *The past does not equal your future unless you allow it to. And prior relationships don't define the script for ones in your future.*

UNLOCK YOUR GREATNESS

In your journal, or using the following pages, write down a few aspirations that move you. These can be anything that serves you. It can be something like, *I am confident. I am beautiful. I am enough. I am strong.* Or perhaps, *Every day in every way I am getting stronger.* Whatever struggle you face, create an empowering affirmation to rewire your mind. Follow the three P's rule: Present Tense, Personal, and Positive. Try saying these affirmations out load, ideally when you're physically moving. There is science behind changing our physical and mental states harmoniously. So perhaps you go for a walk or run first thing in the morning and repeat your affirmations in a melodic way so your body "feels" the words. If you're worried about what other people think, although you shouldn't, use ear plugs so no one will know what you're doing. There is power in the vibration of the spoken word. *Everything is created twice,* first through thought, and then in the physical reality. Therefore, all expressed language, whether through self-talk or conversation with others co-creates your destiny. *Your thoughts become your words. Your words become your actions. Your actions become your habits. Your habits become your character, and your character determines your destiny*[8]

In addition to affirmations, consider the wisdom you've gained from your past. Identify valuable insights and lessons learned from challenging situations or relationships. Reflect on how your experiences have shaped your values, beliefs, and desires. This wisdom can guide you in making more informed choices and empower you to pursue love in alignment with your authentic self. Remember, the journey you've taken has led you to become the beautiful woman you are today.

Then, I'd encourage you to give thought to how you want to celebrate your small successes. It can be the gift of taking personal time to do something you love, but rarely make time for … something that feeds your soul. Simply stated, our behavior is defined by either the desire for pleasure or the need to prevent pain. Our survival brain automatically focuses on either preventing pain or keeping us safe. It is our responsibility to guide our minds to what will bring us fulfillment in alignment with our guiding principles. Following this method will help move you away from simply pursuing short-term pleasures to investing in a longer view of a life that will bring you true fulfillment.

AFFIRMATIONS THAT UPLIFT AND INSPIRE ME

Clarity of mind: Whatever format feels right, I encourage you to journal daily. It will help give you clarity and stops the circling of thoughts in your mind. And it will help to stop the never-ending spiral that typically gets us nowhere. Journaling can help you to forgive and let go of past hurts or regrets. Practicing forgiveness, both towards others and yourself, will help you to release emotional baggage and create a space for new, healthy experiences.

The following are a few key steps that will help you in this journey.

Reflection: Give yourself the time to think about key moments in your past. As I mentioned previously, sometimes the challenges we face offer the greatest opportunity for growth. When reflecting, seek to find the lessons you've learned rather than getting caught up in emotions of the experience. Reflection helps you to appreciate your growth, strengths, and recognize areas for future improvement. As you consider the following questions, remember this isn't about judgement or blame. Try your best to distance yourself from knee jerk reactions to any given circumstance. Be honest with yourself, but not judgmental. The goal is to learn what to let go of and only keep what will serve you.

To practice reflection, you can ask yourself questions like:

- What were the key moments or milestones in my past?
- What were the challenges I faced and how did I overcome them?
- What were the lessons I learned from those experiences?
- How have those experiences shaped me into the woman I am today?
- What skills or knowledge did I gain from those experiences?

By reflecting on your past experiences, you can gain a deeper understanding of yourself, your journey, and become more appreciative of the valuable insights you've acquired along the way.

In this chapter you had a front row seat to reruns of past experiences that may have held you back. You took time to reflect on what each experience has meant to you and then started the process of rewriting the stories you've told yourself over time. By viewing your past through a new lens of lessons learned and gratitude, you should be better equipped to take from your past the wisdom and reflection of growth that will serve you rather than hold you back. And lastly, we discussed how you can use affirmations to instill greater self-confidence. In the next chapter we will explore ways to really integrate self-love and further validate your self-worth. Both are important anchors when seeking to share love again.

EMPOWERMENT FROM WITHIN

Cultivating Self-Love and Self-Worth

"Practicing self-love means learning how to trust ourselves, to treat ourselves with respect, and to be kind and affectionate to ourselves."

- BRENÉ BROWN

According to *Psychology Today*[9], *self-love is a moral value.* Self-love is having regard for our own well-being and contentment according to the *American Psychological Association.*[9] While some may suggest taking baths and getting massages are examples of self-care, loving yourself goes much deeper than splurging periodically on simple pleasures.

Some people may think self-love is akin to narcissism, but self-love is not about having an overinflated sense of self-importance. Self-love means taking caring of your needs, nourishing yourself daily through healthy activities like sound nutrition, exercise, proper sleep, intimacy, and healthy social interactions. It also involves being compassionate with yourself and appreciating your value.

How many times have we seen women, maybe this is you, who from the outside looking in seem to have everything. A successful career, beautiful home, all the trappings and adornments of success, but deep down they're not happy ... something is still missing. Perhaps they struggled to realize success and now believe that being hard on themselves, driving for perfection, led them to succeed. Or maybe they've become embittered because they feel betrayed by men or feel sad about having to navigate life alone. A woman I know is a perfect example. She's become intolerant of failure and unforgiving when or if she falters. The self-scathing commentary and criticism she speaks over herself can make you cringe. We all have critical internal voices. The question is whether you would say the same harsh words to a child or friend. The same tone of compassion and love that we readily extend to others is a gift we should extend to ourselves.

Too often, as women, we set unreasonably high expectations of perfection. The path to becoming our best version is not found through fault-finding narratives. Self-shame and criticism undermine our core as we often look externally for acclamation and support. True love must come from within, so we accept and learn from our failures and celebrate our successes, no matter how small.

Another important thing to please remember, **loving yourself is not selfish;** it simply means you know how to give yourself the love and respect you need and deserve. As women, we're very good at giving to others often with less concern for our own needs. We gain gratitude from making other people feel loved: It's one of our natural gifts. The truth is that we will have more to give to others if we first give to ourselves. How can you achieve deeper self-love? Let's lean into three initial areas before going deeper.

- **_Self-kindness:_** Extend kindness to yourself, replacing criticism, comparison, judgement, or shame. When you speak critical words about yourself, don't follow on by saying more critical things to admonish yourself. This is another endless circle that will only reinforce your negative sentiment. Rewrite the scenario in your mind with a response that is more supportive of your growth. Rather than blurting out comments like, "I'm so stupid," either laugh at yourself or say something that will help you to not repeat the same behavior. No one is perfect and habits take time to break. Although you may think perfection is a worthy goal, perfection is the lowest standard you can pursue, as it's unattainable, and your mind knows that. Accept mistakes as part of your personal growth.

- **_Self-talk and Your Inner Dialogue:_** Words have tremendous power. You deserve to be communicated with in kind and positive ways. The words we use shape our perception of ourselves and the world around us. Think about a time when traffic or technology frustrated you (two easy scenarios for most of us). The slew of negative thoughts and spoken words, some expletives thrown in for good measure to emphatically convey your point, not only put you into a negative mindset, but change your physical state. And that change likely spilled over into other non-related areas of your life.

  Positive and empowering words can boost your self-esteem, foster resilience, and cultivate a positive mindset. Conversely, negative and self-critical words can erode our self-confidence and contribute to feelings of unhappiness. The words we hear and read also influence our perception and perspective on life. Positive and uplifting words can inspire us, motivate us, and instill a sense of hope and optimism. Conversely, negative and discouraging words can dampen our spirits and contribute to a pessimistic outlook. Becoming mindful of our self-talk and what we're letting in is a meaningful form of self-love and self-compassion. We can easily become pawns of social media or the media industry in general. Living from the inside out allows us to control our response. Some examples of a healthier inner dialogue might include: *I walk my own path, and I live with passion. I will have a good day, because I choose to. I am conquering my fears and becoming stronger each day.* Whatever is most meaningful to you, it should be something that can help you reset and become stronger. Whether you consider daily mantras or affirmations, define these words carefully and take the power of words and use it to your benefit.

"No one can make you feel inferior without your consent,"
stated the enlightened Eleanor Roosevelt.

- ***Self-respect:*** Betraying yourself is *the* most harmful form of betrayal. When you choose to dismiss your self-respect by not addressing your emotional needs it's a betrayal of your heart, which cuts deep. Developing healthier self-respect is a transformative journey that involves cultivating a positive relationship with oneself. Show respect for yourself by setting boundaries and prioritizing your needs. Seek to develop a clear understanding of your worth and a commitment to treating yourself with the dignity and respect *you deserve*. This will lay the foundation for healthy relationships, which always starts from within and the relationship you have with yourself. By showing people, whether intimate partners, friends, co-workers, or family members what you will and will not accept, it teaches them how you want to be treated. This is not a prima donna moment, but rather sharing your self-respect with others, which will help them to respect you. This can lead to more fulfilling and long-lasting relationships that are based on mutual respect. There's an old saying; *You can't hold someone accountable for something they don't know.* It's our job, your job, to demonstrate to people in your life how you deserve to be treated based on your values.

Take yourself on a date. I mentioned the book *The Artist's Way* in chapter one. This book was recommended to me by a fellow sculptor; figure sculpting was a passion for me at the time. The concept of taking myself on an "date'" was so foreign. I'd always reserved that term for getting together with a man for dinner or drinks. What I learned was the importance of giving myself time to explore what was soulful to me. I called these times my "stop the world I want to get off" moments. I'd take my camera, get in my car, and just drive, with no specific destination in mind and no expectations as to what I would find. The magic for me was in the journey.

Spending time alone can help to build self-confidence as you may be stepping out of your comfort zone. It sends a powerful message that you value and appreciate yourself enough to invest time and effort into your own well-being and happiness. It allows you to become comfortable with who you are and who you are becoming, independent of others. Personal time also allows for self-discovery. It's an opportunity to reflect on your thoughts, feelings, and experiences. These introspections can lead to a better understanding of who you are, what you value, and what you want in life.

One of my "stop the world I want to get off" explorations involved driving into rural Virginia. Stopping for gas and a bathroom break, I saw a rugged farmer sitting in a rocking chair on the front porch of the general store. I sat down next him, noticed his dirty overalls, big, callous hands and dirty fingernails. His face was etched by time spent in the sun working hard in his fields. His teeth weren't sparkling white; one of his front teeth was missing. I sat there rocking in tandem with him for a few minutes. He looked at me quizzically, not understanding why I was there. After a few more moments, I struck up a conversation with him. He wasn't well educated, eloquent, or refined, but there was a depth of grace, pride, and humility that moved me. I walked away from this man, who didn't meet any of the stereotypes of success, feeling like I was blessed to be in his presence. To share time with someone who may live simply, but did so with pride of family, God, and country, and an appreciation for life's simple gifts. I learned something about myself that day. That living up to societal definitions of success is where many lose their souls; perhaps I was one. This man, who many may have passed by without consideration, made me rethink what is most important. Give yourself the gift of experiencing life, it can sometimes be a mirror into your soul.

Find Your Passion: Be sure to carve out the time for activities that bring you joy and fulfillment. Engaging in hobbies, creative pursuits, or activities that align with your passions helps you to connect with your authentic self and fosters self-love. Passion pursuits challenge you to learn new skills, overcome obstacles, and expand your knowledge and abilities. This journey of continuous growth fosters a sense of fulfillment and accomplishment, contributing to your overall well-being *and* happiness.

Another great benefit you'll enjoy is that hobbies and creative activities can be a form of stress relief and relaxation. One study from the *Society of Behavioral Medicine* suggests that hobbies that you find meaningful lead to fewer negative emotions, which can aid in reducing stress. They provide an outlet for self-expression, allowing you to unwind, recharge, and find comfort in the present moment. I described my feeling when I sculpt of time standing still. Creative pursuits, whatever that means to you, allows you to be in a state of flow. This state of deep concentration and engagement brings a sense of fulfillment and timelessness. It can also cultivate mindfulness, as you become fully present and attuned to the present moment. And, when you engage in activities that align with your passions, you experience a sense of fulfillment and a deeper connection to your values and aspirations.

Meaningless Comparison: As we get older the influence of photoshopped images of perfection often have less impact. But it's still not uncommon for us to compare ourselves to other women. We're bombarded with social media messages and images about what we should do and how we should look as we get older. We're conditioned to be competitive, so comparing ourselves to others seems natural. But for our own happiness, we need to remember that we're all uniquely different and beautiful in our own way! Finding fault by comparing yourself to other women is a waste of time and will only slow you down on your journey to become the *best version of you*. Social media can become an abyss of unrealistic distractions. So often, we see curated and filtered versions of people's lives, which can lead to unrealistic comparisons. Practicing living from the inside out is an important step to cultivating self-acceptance and embracing *your authenticity*. We can do many things to help ourselves feel good about the way we look, but happiness is one of the more effective facial creams. I believe that our biography becomes our biology. If we live with gratitude and positive expectations and focus less on what's wrong and more on what's possible our facial expressions will convey that mental state. Frown lines and lines of discontentment can become etched on our faces. Personally, I'd rather have smile lines.

Celebrate Yourself: I've held onto this belief more strongly as I age. I'm very fortunate to have a handful of friends whose advice and counsel I cherish, whose opinions I respect, and whose support I'll always value and appreciate. Those outside of my inner circle, I'm less concerned about. It's not that I'm indifferent, cold, or less respectful, but their opinions don't influence my life … they don't move the needle.

One of the many gifts of age is we get to the point of not giving a hoot about what other people think, outside of those we cherish. We're less swayed by public opinion. We can, with practice, learn how to focus on our own values. We must maintain our North Star as a guide rather than looking externally for approval, and cherish this liberation from public opinion, as it will serve you. The more you celebrate who you are the stronger you will be as you step into your authentic self.

Protect Your Joy: This is such an important concept! It's too easy to let other people steal your joy. Be selective about the people *you invite* into your life. Protect your energy. There are people, we've probably all known a few, who I call "emotional vampires." They drain you because they care about and only see their needs, not yours. If there's someone who brings toxicity into your life and doesn't take responsibility for their actions, you may need to step away. Genuine confidence and a deep sense of self-worth, not bravado, is something many find threatening if they don't feel the same. I've always believed that life is a dance. Think about all the people you've known over time. Some are intended for a short dance. They appear to teach you a few new steps, perhaps help you to learn something meaningful about yourself. Then there are those who are destined to share a progression of new dances over time. Our challenge is to understand who we should let go and who we should embrace. Don't be afraid. It's liberating and an important part of your journey to let people go, even though it may seem painful.

Always Seek Personal Growth: Bob Proctor stated that, "If we're not growing, we're dying." Beyond this book, I encourage you to continue your personal growth journey. Pursue learning opportunities, set goals that align with your values, and challenge yourself to step outside of your comfort zone. Embracing growth is an investment in your current and future self. One suggestion that you'll find in the accompanying exercise involves writing a personal mission statement. What do you really want out of life and what are your priorities? Your personal mission statement may evolve and change over time, in fact I'd encourage you to revisit this statement periodically, but it's a commitment to yourself. Unlike New Year's resolutions, which often are broken before the end of January, your mission statement should be something more purposeful and guiding. It allows you to really give thought to where you want to direct yourself and your life. A personal mission statement helps you define and clarify *your purpose* in life. It should serve as a guiding compass that aligns your actions, decisions, and goals with your core values and aspirations. It provides a sense of direction and focus, allowing you to make choices that are in line with your true purpose. Ultimately, a personal mission statement will bring a sense of fulfillment and meaning to your life. It allows you to live with intention, knowing that your actions are contributing to something greater than yourself. It provides a sense of fulfillment as you make progress towards your mission and positively impacting the world around you. In fact, perhaps you should consider not only writing, but signing your mission statement. After all, it's a personal creed about how you're going to focus your passion, time, and attention.

Live Intentionally: Did you have a "tada moment" when you read those words? To me, these words sound freeing. What I've learned is that it means making conscious decisions and taking actions that align with my values. Life isn't always easy but will be easier to accept and you will love yourself more, no matter what is happening in your life, when you live with purpose and design. If your intention is to live a meaningful and healthy life, you will make decisions that support this intention, and feel good about yourself when you succeed in this purpose. What you'll experience is that your love of self will grow when you uphold your personal commitments and accomplish what you set out to do. Betraying yourself is deflating and will erode your sense of self-worth. *Living intentionally means you take an active role in creating a life that aligns with your values, passions, and aspirations.* By doing so, you'll experience a greater sense of purpose, fulfillment, and authenticity. To live intentionally based on conscious decisions that support *your happiness*! That's your "tada moment."

Another important way to cultivate self-love is by practicing the art of **mindfulness.**[10] We talked about the value of meditation and focusing our minds. Becoming mindful means being present versus simply reacting to the past or future or what others want from you. It's about developing a clear sense of how you feel, think, and what is important to you. Mindfulness and feeling grateful for who and where you are in life helps to keep you present. It will help you to live consciously rather than reacting to life circumstances as they arise.

For example, self-love is demonstrated when you can turn away from something that feels good and is exciting to what you need to stay strong, centered, and moving forward in your life. By staying focused on what you need, you turn away from automatic behavior patterns that can get you into trouble, keep you stuck in the past, and lessen self-love[11].

The more self-love you feel, the better prepared you are for healthy relationships. Taking another step forward … you will attract people and circumstances to you that support *your* well-being. It's amazing who shows up in your life when you feel confident and truly appreciate and love the woman you are. Have you ever wondered why some men showed up in your life? Perhaps they used you or didn't demonstrate respect for your needs. The real question to ask yourself is whether you attracted these men. Raising your standards is not a one-way street. You need to become the woman that your ideal man will be attracted to. If you're insecure or filled with self-loathing or lack confidence you will give off that energy and attract a predatory man in return. If you don't love and respect yourself, why should he?

A beautiful complement to mindfulness is gratitude as it can help shift your perspective from what is lacking to what is already present in your life. By focusing on blessings, love, and the positives of life, you cultivate a mindset of abundance and appreciation. This shift can create a more positive and open mindset as you navigate the journey to sharing love again.

Another benefit is the natural law of attracting positivity. *Gratitude is a magnet for positive energy.* When you cultivate a sense of gratitude, you emit energy and vibrations that can attract positive experiences and people into your life. By focusing on gratitude, you create an inviting and joyful aura that can enhance your interactions and increases the likelihood of attracting a loving and compatible partner. It's interesting to read this in

Entrepreneur as we may think the discussion about vibration and energy seems too esoteric, but it captures the value perfectly. "As we move through our day, we send energy into the world, and we receive energy back. Our minds, bodies and spirits are composed of energy, which vibrates out and is felt by others. Those vibrations resonate within us and impact our own energy stores."[12]

Focusing on gratitude also helps us to embrace the present moment. If you appreciate what you have in life rather than focusing on what you don't have, it not only elevates your mood, but keeps you present. It helps you to appreciate the journey of finding love rather than solely focusing on the end goal of meeting somebody. By being grateful for the present moment, you can savor the experiences, connections, and personal growth that come along the way.

Part of practicing gratitude should always be to acknowledge and appreciate *yourself* for who you are. This self-acceptance and self-love will naturally radiate outward, making you more attractive and confident in your pursuit of love. The old saying, "confidence is sexy," is so true, but it's confidence that comes from self-love that is most important. Gratitude also helps you to recognize your own worth and value, which is essential in attracting and nurturing a healthy and loving relationship.

Cultivating a positive mindset will influence every aspect of your life. It helps us to focus on the good, even in challenging times. By *training your mind* to seek and appreciate the positive aspects of your life, you develop resilience, optimism, and a positive outlook. A positive mindset naturally supports the natural ups and downs of life.

What you'll experience is that gratitude will foster deeper connections with the people in your life. When you express gratitude towards potential partners, friends, or loved ones, it strengthens the bond that you share and creates a more nurturing relationship. Gratitude also encourages reciprocity, as others are more likely to express their appreciation and love in return. This give and take creates a safe and supportive environment where both parties feel more open to giving *and* receiving. A simple "'thank you" or telling someone how much you honestly appreciate them is like an elixir for their souls. We all want to feel appreciated, respected, and loved.

Incorporating gratitude into your daily life can be as simple as keeping a gratitude journal, expressing gratitude to others, or taking a moment each day to reflect on what you are grateful for. By focusing on gratitude, you cultivate a positive and open heart that can enhance your journey to find love and attract meaningful connections.

Practicing mindfulness and gratitude allows us to be fully present in the moment; to savor the experiences that bring joy and fulfillment. Celebrate the simple pleasures in life and find gratitude in the present moment. By being mindful, you can fully appreciate and celebrate yourself and the experiences you encounter. After all, it is our responsibility to see the grace and gift in each moment.

"Forgiving yourself, believing in yourself and choosing to love yourself are the best gifts one could receive."
Brittany Burgunder, Certified Professional Coach (C.P.C.)

THE ART OF GRATITUDE

Gratitude Journal: Cultivate a gratitude practice by reflecting on and expressing gratitude for the qualities, experiences, and accomplishments that make you unique. Write down three things you're grateful for each day, specifically focusing on aspects about yourself that you truly appreciate.

It's so easy to simply go through life without conscious thought about the paths we venture down. Pause and look around you. There are so many simple things in life for which we can feel a sense of gratitude. Perhaps it was a beautiful sunset or watching a hummingbird at your feeder. It can be a smile shared with a grandchild or random stranger, or a kind gesture demonstrated by the man in your life.

Ideally, take five minutes daily to write in your journal. This practice will allow you to focus and pay attention to the good things in life you might otherwise take for granted. You'll start to find that you become more attuned to everyday sources of pleasure. This shift can be profound. *We can be as happy as we choose or as miserable.* I don't know about you, but I'd rather have a positive mindset that allows me to live life with passion and purpose.

Self-reflection Journaling: Write about your experiences, emotions, and thoughts by scheduling time to journal. Explore your strengths, accomplishments, and areas for growth. Reflect on moments when you felt proud of yourself or when you showed resilience. This exercise helps you recognize your worth and appreciate your journey. Often, we don't give ourselves credit for our accomplishments unless they're monumental. Whereas incremental achievements are the wind in your sails for ongoing momentum.

Another thing to capture in your journal are your small wins. Perhaps you caught yourself about to say something negative or self-deprecating, but you stopped. This progress is worthy of celebration and a personal "high five." Eventually, the times you speak poorly to yourself will lessen, so every positive step *is* a step forward.

There are other ways to cultivate a deeper sense of self-love. I'll offer three other considerations that you can try at different times. Again, we're all unique, so perhaps certain suggestions may seem uncomfortable. Part of our growth is moving beyond our comfort zone, so I encourage you to try each one, but you may settle on the one or two that resonate with you. You can always come back to the other suggestions at some future time.

- ***Mirror Work:*** This is often difficult but stand in front of a mirror and look into your eyes. Speak words of love, acceptance, and encouragement to yourself. Affirm your worth, acknowledge your strengths, and express gratitude for your journey. This exercise can make you feel vulnerable, but it can be incredibly powerful.

  Perhaps you've done something similar in the past. You studied yourself in the mirror after you've let yourself down or found yourself repeating a past mistake. Rather than looking into your soul to ask *why again* this time express love for who you are.

- ***Evidence Journal:*** Sometimes it is helpful to write down the evidence of self-worth. Our minds can find negatives as easily as it can find positive reinforcements. As you challenge disempowering beliefs be sure to write down the "evidence" of times when you've done the same thing or demonstrated the behavior well. Reminding yourself of your wins and the occasions when you proved that the change your seeking is within you, the easier it will become to start demonstrating those behaviors more consistently.

- ***Self-care Rituals:*** Engage in regular self-care activities that nourish your mind, body, and soul. This can include activities like taking relaxing baths, practicing mindfulness, or meditation, going for walks in nature, or indulging in hobbies that bring you joy. Prioritizing self-care is an act of self-love so make it a *non-negotiable* part of your routine.

- ***Setting Boundaries:*** Practice setting and maintaining healthy boundaries in your relationships and daily life. Learn to say "no" to things that don't align with your values or drain your energy. Prioritize your needs and well-being and communicate those needs with confidence. Setting boundaries is an act of self-respect and self-worth. This is especially important for women as we tend to allow our boundaries to be stretched by partners and family members. We can still be supportive, kind, and loving without losing sight of what makes us feel whole.

- ***Surrounding Yourself with Positivity:*** Surround yourself with people, environments, and external influences like social media that uplift and inspire you. Seek out supportive and loving relationships that encourage your growth. Engage in activities that align with your passions and values. Surrounding yourself with *positivity* nourishes your self-worth and reinforces self-love. It also counteracts our natural tendencies to focus on those things that could cause us pain … which can make us feel stressed and less in control. I've mentioned this idea of "training" our minds. It's something worth really thinking about because we need to consciously monitor what comes in and what comes out of our minds. If we keep exposing ourselves to negative people and thoughts, we can't expect anything else but a negative responsive and ultimately, a negative outlook. *Feed your mind with intent.*

Another exercise I'd like to propose for you is to create a *Personal Mission Statement.* It doesn't need to be perfect; it can be modified whenever it serves you. What's more important is that you give meaningful thought to your life mission and aspirations.

I'M UNIQUE AND BEAUTIFUL!

MY PERSONAL MISSION STATEMENT

In this chapter, we highlighted the importance of self-love and how it differs from selfishness, and often allows us to be more selfless. By filling our own emotional reservoir, we have more to give. Living in the moment and practicing mindfulness and gratitude can help you to realize and attract greater positivity. Positivity in both life circumstances and the type of people who will be attracted *to you.*

Please keep in mind that, as with any self-development effort, cultivating self-love and self-worth is an ongoing practice. Be patient and compassionate with yourself throughout the journey. *Embrace your uniqueness, celebrate your strengths, and honor your worth. You deserve love, happiness, and a deep sense of self-acceptance!*

In the next chapter we'll start to consider our desires and relationship goals. With a greater sense of self and a stronger core guided by self-worth, this chapter helps you to reflect on what you're looking for in a relationship. With a deeper appreciation of who you are authentically, taking from your past those gifts and wisdom which will serve you, we now want to give thought to your goals for a new relationship.

CHAPTER FIVE

GREATER CLARITY

Aligning Relationship Goals with Self-Worth Wisdom

"You are never too old to set another goal or to dream a new dream."

– C.S. LEWIS

Before we delve into this chapter, I'd like to share a story, which in retrospect seems so silly, but perhaps you can relate. If not, it's embarrassing. Several years ago, a girlfriend and I were having a glass of wine at a local restaurant in Annapolis. We were sharing our latest disappoints with men we had met online or through friends. So, we decided to write what our ideal man should look like, on our bar napkins. The list included things like: He didn't snore, he was trustworthy, athletic … the list was extensive, covered both sides of our napkins, and included our want-to-haves and must-haves and … our deal breakers. I think back on this night and laugh. It was such a superfluous list. It was fun, but in many ways, it was a simple exercise that held no meaning. Finding true love, someone who is aligned with who you have become, is a much deeper exercise. I think we can all agree on this point.

Clarifying your desires and relationship goals is an essential step in the self-discovery process when seeking love. It allows you to gain a deeper understanding of what you *truly want and need* in a relationship, which can guide you to finding a fulfilling relationship with a compatible partner (replacing the proverbial list on a bar napkin). Here are a few reasons why clarifying your desires and relationship goals is so important,

Self-awareness is invaluable when we invest the time needed to reflect on our desires and relationship goals. This means understanding your values, priorities, and *what you bring to a relationship*. Remember, likes attract likes. It helps you to identify what you're looking for in a partner and what kind of relationship aligns with your authentic self. It's about not compromising your values, but rather feeling empowered. To believe that you deserve to share yourself, your heart, body and soul, with someone who is your equal. Someone who will *contribute* to your life and support and share in your continued growth, as you will in theirs.

Focus and Intention: Clarifying your desires and relationship goals helps you focus your energy and intention on finding a compatible partner. It allows you to be more selective and discerning in your dating journey, ensuring that you invest your time and emotional energy in relationships that have the potential to meet your needs and aspirations.

Unfortunately, so many women when they pass the age of 50 feel like they have fewer meaningful choices when it comes to men. This is often true of younger women as well, I might add. Personally, I believe this is far from the truth. If we're authentic, feel and act youthful, confident, and self-assured there's no reason to believe we can't attract a mature and emotionally healthy man. Some men will always gravitate to younger women to satisfy their own insecurities, but there are many men who enjoy spending time with an emotionally mature woman who brings less drama to their lives. Someone they can more closely relate to with shared commonalities about their past.

Avoid Settling: When you have a clear understanding of your desires and relationship goals, you are less likely to settle for less than what you deserve. It empowers you to set healthy boundaries, recognize red flags, and make choices that align with your long-term happiness and fulfillment. We'll focus more on red flags in a bit. Although many are self-evident a quick refresh never hurts as you venture forth into the dating world.

Effective Communication: Communication can be a chapter in and of itself, but let's start the conversation. Knowing your desires and relationship goals enables you to communicate them effectively to potential partners. This type of open and honest communication fosters understanding, builds trust, and helps you find someone who shares your vision for a fulfilling relationship. If you don't have a vision, it will prove difficult to find someone who is aligned. It's like the old saying, "If you don't know where you're going, how will you know if you arrived?" You both need to be on the same page for things to work well.

Personal Growth: Clarifying your desires and relationship goals is a journey of self-discovery that can lead to personal growth. It allows you to explore your own needs, desires, and boundaries, which in turn helps you to become more self-assured and confident in your pursuit of love.

So how do you clarify your relationship goals? This is a question that is unique to you. In the accompanying exercises, I encourage you to take the time to reflect, journal and explore what truly *matters to you* in a relationship. A relationship should be an addition to your life, so think of this as an opportunity to grow, learn, and attract the love *you deserve.* Although every relationship has its moments as you're getting to know one another, it shouldn't feel like a constant struggle. I remember a relationship where it was such a roller coaster ride. There was a strong connection, but not a healthy one. We both pursued the relationship based on what was missing in our lives and in ourselves. We were forcing something that shouldn't have been, so it became an emotional drain. I realized in time that I was trying to recapture my past. I wasn't grounded in the present and hadn't taken the time to go through the process of self-reflection to really grow into the woman I am today. The time wasted in situations and relationships that don't serve us is time we'll never recapture. Not every relationship will be perfect, but setting yourself up for success will increase your odds of happiness and allow you to not waste precious moments with men who aren't well aligned.

WHAT DO YOU REALLY WANT?

What are you really looking for in a relationship? The following exercises will help you to get a clearer picture.

Journaling: Set aside dedicated time to journal about your desires and relationship goals. Write freely and without judgment, allowing your thoughts and feelings to flow onto the pages. Earlier in the book, we also discussed journaling, but we went through honoring your past, which likely included past relationships. The wisdom that you gained in each situation can be your future roadmap. Reflect on what you truly want in a relationship, your values, and the kind of partner you envision. It's also helpful to visualize the type of relationship you want. Explore your aspirations, dreams, and any patterns or preferences you've noticed in past relationships. View this vision through the lens of the stronger, more confident and focused you. Try not to default to statements like, "Anyone but." If you find yourself going down this path, you may want to revisit honoring and letting go of whatever past relationship or experience you automatically defaulted to for comparison.

Create a Vision Board: This is a great exercise for those of you who are visual. Gather magazines, images, and words that resonate with your desires and relationship goals. Create a visual representation of what you want to manifest in your life and the life you'd like to share with a new partner. Arrange these images on a board or in a digital collage. Display it somewhere you can see it regularly, allowing it to serve as a reminder and inspiration for your relationship aspirations. Even the process of gathering images and words can be insightful. You'll notice that you automatically gravitate to certain words and pictures.

Ask Yourself Questions: These should be thought-provoking questions to delve deeper into your desires and relationship goals. A couple of examples may include:

- What are my core values and how do they align with my desired relationship?
- What qualities and characteristics do I seek in a partner? Do they align with my own values and aspirations?
- Do I possess the similar qualities and characteristics that would attract the man I'd like to meet?
- What are my long-term relationship goals? Do I envision a committed partnership or marriage?
- What are my non-negotiables in a relationship?
- What boundaries do I need to establish to make sure I protect my well-being, happiness, and ongoing growth?
- What have I learned from past relationships? How can I apply those lessons to shape my future relationship goals?
- What are my emotional needs and how can they be supported in a healthy and fulfilling relationship?
- How do I want us to communicate and resolve conflicts?
- Are there things I still need to work on to help foster healthy communication?
- What role does personal growth and individual autonomy play in my future relationship?
- How can I support my partner's growth while nurturing my own?
- How do I envision shared values, interests, and goals with a partner? How important is it for us to have common ground in these areas?
- How do I want to feel in a relationship? What emotional connection and support do I desire from a partner?
- Do I know anyone who has a healthy and loving relationship? If so, are there things I could learn from speaking with them?

These questions are meant to be examples to get you started. This is *your* self-reflection and exploration. Take your time to answer whatever questions are most important to you honestly and authentically. Your relationship goals and aspirations may evolve over time, so it's important to regularly revisit and reassess them as you grow and learn more about yourself. Your journal can be an ideal retrospect of your thoughts over time.

Another idea to consider is to get an outside perspective. Ask some of your trusted friends or family members to provide *objective* insights. But before you go down this path, I encourage you to view this time as a forward-thinking exercise versus a rehash of the past with cheerleaders who are viewing this exercise through the lens of the "old you." Openly share your thoughts and feelings about your desires and relationship goals and listen to their feedback and observations. Sometimes, an outside perspective can shed light on aspects you may not have considered. It may also highlight areas of personal growth that still need your attention.

Self-reflection and Meditation: Set aside quiet time for self-reflection and meditation. Perhaps start with a simple question and let your mind be still. Pay attention to your intuition and listen to the whispers of your heart. Allow yourself to connect with your deepest desires and relationship goals without external distractions. This gift, like journaling, allows you to get below the noise. Eventually, the voices of self-doubt or personal reprisal subside. We hear the voice of intuition and learn what is most important.

These exercises are meant to be personal and introspective. So often, we simply jump back into dating (a friend suggests you should try Bumble, Match, or Our Time) and you find yourself saying, "Yes," or "Maybe." Of course, there are some women who sit completely on the sidelines and only talk about their desire to meet someone (but do nothing). Taking the first step can be done in confidence if you've gone through the steps we just explored together. You'll find that you're starting to really understand yourself and who you're looking to meet and the type of relationship you want to share. So, take your time, be patient with yourself, and embrace the process of self-discovery. As you gain clarity about your desires and relationship goals, you'll be better equipped to attract and cultivate healthy relationships. Always ask yourself whether the focus aligns with your North Star. This will help to keep you grounded and focused on the meaningful aspects of meeting men.

Dr. Christina Hibbert explains this about self-esteem and self-worth: "Self-esteem is what we think and feel and believe about ourselves. Self-worth is recognizing 'I am greater than all of those things.' It is a deep knowing that I am of value, that I am lovable, necessary to this life, and of incomprehensive worth." I am enough!

Which is why your self-worth and self-value are such critical elements to finding a loving and healthy relationship. Many of us let our self-worth be contingent upon external events. As a result, our feelings about ourselves end up being at the whim of the world.[13] We discussed cultivating self-love in the last chapter. As we continue to develop a greater sense of our worth, it's helpful to highlight some additional points. You'll notice that this is a building block approach. As you strengthen yourself in one area, you're better prepared to move forward.

- ***Knowing your worth translates into recognizing your inherent value as an individual.*** It involves having a healthy level of self-esteem and self-confidence, which are attractive qualities that can enhance your interactions with potential partners. When you know your worth, you exude self-assurance and are less likely to settle for less than you deserve. ***Confidence is sexy***. Feeling self-assured, being comfortable in your own skin, is a quality most men find incredibly attractive. And I'm talking about emotionally healthy men. Men who aren't emotionally healthy, whether controlling or insecure, love women who don't feel worthy. They feed off this lack of confidence and self-worth. Perhaps not consciously, as many who behave this way don't possess high emotional IQs, but you'll bear the brunt of their lack of emotional health, nonetheless.

- *Understanding your worth empowers you* to set and maintain healthy boundaries in relationships. You recognize what you will and won't tolerate, *and* you communicate your needs and expectations clearly. This helps to create a foundation of respect and mutual understanding, fostering healthier and more fulfilling connections.

- *When you know your worth, you become a magnet for partners who appreciate and value you for who you are.* By embodying self-respect and self-love, you naturally attract individuals who are compatible with your values and treat you with the love and respect you deserve. Bravado and the diva dance are not authentic and will likely only attract the type of men who are easily swayed by surface behaviors that are flaunted to be genuine.

Knowing your worth, deeply appreciating your value, acts as a shield against toxic relationships. It helps you to recognize red flags and avoid getting involved with partners who can undermine your self-esteem or try to manipulate your emotions. When you have a strong sense of self-worth, you are less likely to tolerate mistreatment or settle for unhealthy dynamics. Perhaps you thought about an unhealthy relationship when you went through the *Legacy of Resilience* chapter. Reflecting on the reasons *why* certain men came into your life and *how* the relationship unfolded should provide tremendous insight about what worked and what didn't. What red flags could you have recognized if you were more grounded or felt a greater sense of self-worth? No judgements here. It's about understanding your past, so you don't repeat behaviors that don't align with your deepened self-worth.

Understanding your worth is an ongoing journey of self-discovery and personal growth. The beauty of Rome was not built in a day. This process involves continuously learning about yourself, your strengths, and your areas for improvement. By investing in your personal development, you enhance your self-worth and become a better partner in relationships. And you'll find greater happiness overall.

Remember, knowing your worth is not about arrogance or entitlement. It's about celebrating *your own value,* embracing self-love, and cultivating healthy relationships based on mutual respect and appreciation. *Trust yourself, honor your needs, and believe that you deserve love and happiness.* Step into a better version of yourself and you'll attract a man who has already become a better version of himself ... or is at least well down a similar path.

Red Flags: Any discussion about pursuing love again should include a section on identifying red flags. Being confident in your self-worth and self-love will empower you to recognize the incongruence of certain behaviors with what you want and deserve. Unfortunately, we've all likely accepted or ignored red flags as being *part of the package* rather than warning signals, so let's do a quick refresh on things to watch for.

- ***Controlling Behavior:*** Men who try to control your movements, decisions, or beliefs are more concerned about *their needs* and what *they want.* This type of behavior does not support a healthy relationship.

- ***Lack of Trust:*** We've talked about the importance of trust; it's one of the tenets of a healthy relationship. When a partner distrusts you or doesn't believe you'll do the right thing, that can be a sign. It's likely more about his insecurities and inability to trust than your actions.

- ***Low Self-esteem:*** Someone who loves you should also want to support you. In a healthy relationship, you're a cheerleader for your partner as well as yourself. Unfortunately, there are men who knock a woman down to feel stronger and more in control. If you experience this . . . run! This type of behavior is a form of emotional abuse.

- ***Substance Abuse:*** Often, this behavior represents a person who struggles with impulse control and self-destructive habits. Our compassion may get the better of us if we're not careful. I've seen women lose themselves in the struggle to help someone who doesn't want to help themselves.

- ***Anger Management:*** I'm not sure how much explanation is needed here. In a healthy relationship, you should feel safe tackling difficult subjects without fear of intimidation or worse. Flying off the handling demonstrates a lack of self-control. I'm not talking about the occasional outburst, but repeated and excessive anger that elicits a visceral response from you that you find unnerving.

- ***Codependency:*** Perhaps less likely to be an issue for a mature and secure woman, but something to touch on. If a man relies on you too much or exclusively for emotional and psychological support or suffocates you, your time, and emotional energy, that is a sign. This type of individual will not only exhaust you but will stunt your personal growth.

- ***Gaslighting:*** This behavior is an insidious form of emotional abuse in which the manipulator will make you question your own sanity or judgement. Gaslighting is another form of controlling behavior that can erode your self-esteem overtime.

- ***Constant Jealousy:*** I've known women who have alienated themselves from friends and family members due to being with a man who is threatened by them spending time with other important people in their life. Again, suffocating behaviors are not healthy for us. Our worlds should expand as we grow.

- ***Lack of Emotional Intelligence:*** *The* beauty of becoming a stronger version of yourself is that you'll easily recognize this behavior. People with a low level of emotional intelligence are unable to pick up on your feelings or empathize with you. This often results in unnecessary conflicts or forms of manipulation.

With that list on the table, let's move on to discussing the power of intuition and how it can serve you. It's interesting that as we grow older, we often develop a keener sense of intuition. *We've learned over time to trust ourselves.* Trusting your instincts is a valuable quality when seeking love again. What is intuition? It's the ability to understand or know something without needing to think about it or use reason to discover it. It's the ability to understand something without the need for conscious reasoning.

Your instincts, or intuition, can be a powerful guiding force when it comes to matters of the heart. It's that gut feeling or inner voice that provides insights and guidance beyond logical reasoning. Trusting your instincts means listening to that inner wisdom and allowing it to inform your decisions and choices in the realm of love. I don't know if this is true for you, but as an adult, the times I chose to ignore my inner voice were the times I got myself in trouble. Over the years, I've learned to reflect and cultivate this intuitive sense.

Your instincts can also help you to recognize red flags or warning signs early, which is crucial when starting a relationship. At this point in our lives, let's not waste time hoping that someone will change for the better and no longer demonstrate the red flags that he's giving off. I obviously believe in personal growth and development, but the investment of time and energy is an individual pursuit. We should continue to grow with our partners, but I would suggest our future partner should not come to the table expecting or needing a complete overhaul. Here are some tips for women to identify potential red flags, like the ones outlined above.

Trust Your Intuition: Pay close attention to your gut feelings. If something feels off or doesn't sit right with you, it's important to acknowledge and explore those feelings not to dismiss them. Your intuitive sense is something you cultivated over time, not a knee jerk response based on a past issue that you've not reconciled. Sit quietly and let your inner voice speak to you. As you continue to distance yourself from the past and move forward with the lessons and wisdom gained, you'll find that your inner voice becomes less reactionary and more insightful.

Observe Their Behavior: Watch how your potential partner treats others, especially those in service positions or people over which they may have authority. It can be a good indicator of their character and how they may treat *you* in the future. One of my dating rules was if a man was rude and arrogant when dealing with a server simply to demonstrate his authority, he didn't deserve another date.

Communication Patterns: Notice how they communicate with you. Do they listen actively, respect your boundaries, and respond in a timely manner? Healthy communication is vital for a successful relationship. A dating test that recently went viral on social media is called the *Bird Test*. The premise is that when you see a beautiful bird and mention it to your partner how does he respond? Does he acknowledge, look, and appreciate what you find to be beautiful or does he ignore or brush it off? The basis of this simple test is whether he's engaged and interested in what interests you.

Consistency: Look for consistency in their words and actions. If they frequently make promises but fail to follow through, it could be a red flag for future reliability and trust issues. Sometime who spins a nice tale without depth is less likely to be worthy of your attention.

Respect and Boundaries: Really pay attention to how they respect your boundaries and personal space. If they consistently disregard your boundaries or make you feel uncomfortable, it's important to address it early on. If they're unable to respect your self-respect there's an issue. See how they treat other family members, especially their mother. I dated a man for a brief time who was so rude and profane when speaking with his mother. I'm not saying this is tried and true, but it gave me pause and it turned out to be a legitimate red flag. The lack of respect he demonstrated to his mother started to come through pretty early in our relationship.

Control and Possessiveness: Be cautious of signs of excessive control or possessiveness. Healthy relationships are built on trust and mutual respect, not control or manipulation. We discussed some of the red flags involved with this behavior such as jealousy, possessiveness, and not respecting your boundaries. But here is something to consider that we may easily overlook. Be wary of a man who pushes for a fast-paced and intense relationship, declaring love or commitment early on. It may seem very flattering, but this can be a tactic to establish control and prevent you from having time to assess the relationship objectively. I experienced this behavior first-hand with my ex-husband. He swept me off my feet quickly and pushed for a rapid progression of our relationship so he could wield control. As I was feeling vulnerable and insecure at the time, just coming off my illness, I didn't recognize the signs.

We know it's important to take our time when getting to know someone: Your instincts can certainly help. Sometimes, your intuition picks up on subtle clues or inconsistencies that your conscious mind may overlook. By trusting your instincts, you can protect yourself from potentially harmful or unhealthy relationships and make more informed decisions about who to pursue a deeper connection with. Intuition, coupled with personal reflection, can help you to identify whether a potential partner aligns with your core values, beliefs, goals, and desires. Your instincts can guide you to individuals who resonate with your authentic self, fostering a more genuine connection and increasing the likelihood of a fulfilling relationship.

Trusting your instincts reflects self-awareness and self-trust. It means having confidence in your own judgment and honoring your inner wisdom. By cultivating this trust in self, you become more empowered in your pursuit of love and are better equipped to make choices that align with your long-term happiness and well-being.

Trusting your instincts and embracing vulnerability often go hand in hand. It means being open to the possibility of love and allowing yourself to be guided by your emotional intelligence and intuition. We all know there are no guarantees in matters of the heart, but trusting your instincts can help you to navigate the uncertainties and take meaningful steps towards finding love again.

It's all about finding a balance between rationality and intuition and using both to make informed decisions in your pursuit of love. The key is to trust yourself, listen to your inner voice, and have faith that your instincts will guide you down the right path.

In this chapter we drilled down on what you're really looking for in a relationship and what the qualities and characteristics are of the man you feel would be suitable. We discussed how your intuition can be a helpful guide when reflecting on the qualities and characteristics of a man with whom you're considering sharing time. In the next chapter we'll discuss the value of opening yourself up to being vulnerable on the path to enjoying greater emotional intimacy.

CHAPTER SIX

HEARTFELT CONNECTIONS

Embracing Vulnerability for Deeper Emotional Intimacy

"Vulnerability is the courage to be yourself in a world that constantly tries to shape you."

- KAMAND KOJOURI

The word *vulnerability* can mean different things to different people. Some, view it as a sign of weakness or loss of control. Others view it as the foundation to share themselves more openly. I'd like to encourage you to view vulnerability as a willingness to show up authentically, to be seen and heard, and to take emotional risks. Being vulnerable involves embracing uncertainty, discomfort, and the possibility of rejection or disappointment. But what you'll find is that embracing vulnerability is the pathway to deeper connections.

I've watched my mother, over time, become stronger and more openly expressive. Raised in the UK, she was typically more reserved. She realized after my father passed that being vulnerable and expressive brought people closer to her. That she was able to connect more authentically and enjoy deeper relationships.

Brené Brown, an American Professor, author, and podcast host, speaks so eloquently on the feelings of vulnerability, shame, and empathy. In one podcast, she highlights the underlying reason why so many people shy away from vulnerability: the fear that they're not enough. It takes courage to be openly imperfect. In her latest book, *Dare to Lead,*[14] she mentions, "Wherever perfectionism is driving us, shame is riding shotgun."

It takes a well of compassion to be kind to ourselves first. And it takes inner strength to take emotional risks, and to step in when you're scared, to be willing to say something first. Perhaps, "I love you." But letting ourselves be deeply seen is such an important step if we're to experience love deeply with someone worthy. Trust and vulnerability, when shared, allows you to realize greater depths of personal connection.

Soon after meeting my love, Mark, he asked if I wanted to share an adventure of traveling on a boat going from Annapolis, Maryland to Florida. We were to travel down the Intercoastal Waterway on a lovely forty-four foot powerboat and then cut across Florida on the Okeechobee. An amazing adventure without question, but I barely knew him; we had only been dating a short time. I heard myself saying, "Yes," when he asked, then looking around seeing if someone else was in the room. All kidding aside, I was to share a small space for months where no ambiguities or imperfections could be hidden. It took courage, a strong intuition, and trust in my personal judgement that he aligned with my values. It took belief that he was worthy and a belief that I was enough. Being in close quarters forced us to address emotional triggers and learn how to communicate our needs in a speed dating fashion. The extensive time I'd spent learning about myself allowed me to navigate this relationship and to help Mark in the process since he was recently divorced. We grew together during our trip, something we still prioritize and enjoy years later.

Embracing vulnerability is powerful and transformative. To help you feel more comfortable letting down some of your barriers and being more open, here are some key points to consider.

Boundaries: Have you ever felt in a relationship that your man overstepped his place? I think we've all felt that way at some point in our lives. It's important to set healthy boundaries in relationships, so we don't start stacking resentment about his actions. As a mature woman seeking a partner, you should prioritize your own well-being to ensure that your needs and boundaries are respected. This includes communicating your expectations and desires openly and honestly. If done in a mutually respectful and mature way, it allows your new partner to understand you more fully and be more supportive. It's unfair to hold him accountable for something you've not shared. Give him a key to understanding what's important to you.

Beliefs and Assumptions: Similar to the exercise that focused on rewriting personal stories, it's valuable to understand your beliefs and assumptions in all areas of your life—whether about yourself, others, or the world around you. This clarity will give you confidence to reconsider or pivot to a new perspective. This can be especially important if a limiting belief is holding you back. For example, if you believe that men in your age bracket are only attracted to young women with perfect figures, you'll likely feel insecure and may question the man's motives. By having the confidence to challenge these beliefs you can adopt more empowering ones that serve you. This self-reflection can open you up to new possibilities. We'll delve into this in deeper detail in the following exercise.

Noticing Patterns and Triggers: How do you define an emotional trigger? According to *Psychology Today,*[15] an emotional trigger is simply any topic that makes you feel uncomfortable. Triggers can represent past situations and wounds. When you know your emotional triggers, you can take actionable steps to take care of yourself and develop a stronger inner voice to help navigate you through these uncomfortable situations. Perhaps you hit a couple of triggers when you were reflecting on your past. We all have them. Unfortunately, unless we consciously understand and work through these triggers, they will pop up again.

Try to observe your recurring thoughts, emotions, and behaviors. By doing so, you can make *conscious choices* for personal growth rather than simply reacting in the moment.

The truth is, there are no *negative* emotions because they all serve a purpose, but we should seek to understand our emotions so we can control them and ultimately our destiny. Let's delve into a few steps you can follow.

- ***Identify the Emotion.*** For example, do you feel frustrated, sad, or angry? Understanding your emotional state can be a valuable message. It's the starting point for you. We can learn to change our emotional state. How we respond to things is a choice–an empowering statement that we should all take to heart as it will help us to realize that we can change.

- ***Think About the Message:*** Step back to consider the signs. Consider what just happened and the response it activated within you.

- ***Trace the Roots:*** Perhaps there were similar situations from your past that made you feel the same way. We all have baggage at this stage in our lives. Perhaps your ex was dismissive or unappreciative of how beautiful you looked after you spent time getting ready for date night. And the man you're now dating innocently says something that triggers the same feeling of not being good enough. How do you react?

- ***Seek to Understand:*** Sometimes, you'll need to dig a bit deeper. Strong emotions that easily flare should be viewed through the lens of curiosity not judgement or reprisal. Don't try to ignore them or fight them back–it doesn't work. Instead, try to think about what might have triggered this response. Owning your emotions allows you to approach change. Give yourself credit for acknowledging the differences between your past and present–that you're creating that difference. This reminder can help you to take back control, your power, and actively choose a different response.

- ***Honoring Your Past:*** This is something you'll likely revisit multiple times as you get into a new relationship. Be patient. Sometimes it's helpful to share with your partner that your response was based on something in your past. If we feel a person is aware that their response was not aligned to the situation, and they're in the process of rewiring how they respond, we're much more likely to be understanding and supportive.

- ***Be Open:*** Some people in our lives may be socially unaware of their actions, so it's helpful to remember that most people aren't trying to hurt you on purpose. Some of their actions or words that you find upsetting may represent some of their emotional triggers. I spent five months on a boat with a man I'd been dating for only a short time. Being in close quarters, 24/7, forced us both to navigate through our trigger points. Mark was recently divorced, so his emotions and triggers were closer to the surface, but I had my own baggage to reconcile. This is where an emotional pause is so important as it gives us time to gather our thoughts so we can communicate constructively. If you've ever read Stephen Covey's *Seven Habits of Highly Effective People*, he talks about the space or pause between the situation (stimuli) and the response. The pause is where you give yourself a moment to *choose* your response. Too often, when we are in reactionary mode, we blurt things out in self-defense. We may feel badly or even foolish, but we can't take back what was just said in the heat of the moment. The more you practice using your pause button when you feel a little unsteady or a little emotionally reactive the easier it will become for you, and your partner.

The "V" Word: Vulnerability is not about being perfect or having all the answers. It's liberating to embrace your imperfections and extend grace and compassion to yourself in the process! Vulnerability gives you space for growth, learning, and the opportunity to connect on a deeper level with others. Think of vulnerability as a strength rather than a weakness. When you develop that inner confidence that your imperfections are part of what makes you uniquely wonderful, you're able to share more of you, the real you.

Acknowledge that it takes strength for you to embrace vulnerability. It's much easier to put up barriers and hide behind them. So, celebrate small acts of courage when you step into being vulnerable, no matter how small these acts may seem. We're not always our best cheerleaders. Positive reinforcement increases our willingness to be vulnerable and encourages further growth. If you stumble, that's okay. Give yourself the grace of forgiveness and the gift of trying again.

Emotional Intimacy: Let's move on to a vital aspect of any healthy and fulfilling relationship, regardless of age or gender. Sharing emotional intimacy can be wonderful, perhaps scary, but wonderful, nonetheless.

Emotional intimacy involves a deep connection and understanding between partners. It goes beyond surface-level interactions and allows you to truly know and be known by your partner. Your unique journey, life events, and personal growth, can all contribute to a deeper emotional connection with a partner who appreciates and values your uniqueness.

Women who have been hurt or disappointed in the past, which is likely most of us, often struggle with emotional intimacy as it requires a willingness to be vulnerable and open with your partner. It means sharing your thoughts, feelings, fears, and dreams in a safe and supportive environment. That's why it's important to go through the steps involved with authenticity, accepting the wisdom from past experiences, and embracing self-love. This core understanding is part of your foundation. A greater sense of self-awareness and self-acceptance will help you to create a deeper level of vulnerability and emotional connection in your relationships. Think about people you know who share a strong marriage or bond with their partner versus those who don't. In less emotionally intimate relationships, we often witness them nipping at each other's heels. Some will try to belittle their partner in front of others to get their point across and take control. Or they sit around and complain about their partner to their friends rather than taking ownership so that they can contribute to the improvement of their relationship.

Here is another reason why daily journaling can be so beneficial. When you see your fears written on paper it helps you to gain clarity . . . you can emotionally take a step back. Perhaps your fear of vulnerability is genuine given your partner, but maybe your fear is just a reflection of your past. When we write things down, it removes it from the spiraling thought process that goes on within our minds. It helps us to see patterns, to understand the cause and the underlying truth. Another important step that can help you gain clarity is solitude. Spending time with your own thoughts allows you to see your imperfections. Not to pass judgement, but to be aware. *This prepares us to love someone else, in all their beauty and imperfection.*

The phrase, *having each other's back* is one often used today. Mutual support and empathy means being there for each other during both the joys and challenges of life. Having clear boundaries and a definite sense of self allows you to talk about what you and your partner need without judgement or criticism. Being authentic will encourage the same reciprocal behavior. If we're good people, we want to help and support those we love guided by the insights of what we know is important to them.

There's so much to say about how to communicate. We touched on this in a prior chapter. Strong and open communication skills provide a solid foundation for any relationship, but one could argue it's even more important when intimacy is involved. You don't want to guess or feel unsteady about where someone stands. Have you ever known someone who simply couldn't express how they were feeling yet held you accountable for the knowledge they couldn't share? It's frustrating. Perhaps you felt like you were often walking on eggshells around them. Not a healthy foundation for any relationship. *Being able to openly communicate and share your thoughts is an example of self-worth: We believe that our needs and feeling are important and therefore want to have open and healthy dialogues.* Before we discuss the *how* of effective communication, let's explore how communication is linked to emotional intimacy and why it's so important.

- ***Effective communication helps set the stage for building trust in a relationship.*** When partners communicate openly, honestly, and authentically, it fosters trust and creates a safe space for emotional intimacy to flourish. Both partners are encouraged to be communicative and open about their feelings.
- ***Communication is the vehicle through which emotions and needs are expressed.*** Emotional intimacy requires partners to feel comfortable sharing their feelings, desires, and concerns. Open and honest communication allows for a deeper understanding of each other's emotional worlds. We all have a private sense of self. *To help your partner to be supportive and understanding we need to let them in.*
- ***Communication involves not only expressing oneself but also actively listening and empathizing to what the other person is saying.*** When partners actively listen, they show genuine interest, validate each other's emotions, and seek to understand the other's perspective. This level of empathy and engagement deepens

emotional intimacy and strengthens the bond shared between partners. Think about a time when you were sharing something you felt was important and the other person interrupted, was dismissive, or simply wasn't paying attention. How did that make you feel? If I were to guess, I'd say, "not so good." Not feeling important, heard, or respected by your partner will erode trust over time. Sometimes we neglect to engage because we're distracted. He may not have meant to be dismissive. Healthy communication, rather than wielding a caustic response, will help the other person to understand what he may have done "wrong." Of course, this is a two-way street.

- ***Conflict and disagreements are natural … it's how we handle them that will define a relationship.*** Understanding the tenets of good communication facilitates healthy and constructive resolution to issues that may naturally come up in any relationship. Screaming at each other in the heat of the moment, one would argue, is not constructive. When partners communicate respectfully, assertively, and with a focus on understanding and finding solutions, it promotes emotional intimacy. Conflict resolution allows for the expression of differing opinions and needs while maintaining a sense of connection and understanding. Sometimes, we so want to get our point across it's hard to stop and simply listen. While our partner is speaking, we're already outlining our response because we have such a great point, our defense, to share. This is when our pause button is so helpful. When Mark and I disagree, we give each other time to present our side or view without interruption. It took practice, but the result is so much better. Both of us feel heard and we can constructively decide to agree to disagree or come to a happy medium. Either way, both of us walk away feeling good about the end point. We don't allow a minor disagreement to be blown out of proportion based solely on how we shared our thoughts or didn't listen.

- *Another value to cultivating strong communication skills is it helps partners to create a shared meaning about their relationship.* Through an open and ongoing dialogue, partners can align their values, goals, and visions for the future. This shared meaning fosters emotional intimacy by creating a sense of unity and purpose. You're now a couple working together on the realization of goals that are mutually beneficial and exciting.

- *Honest and open communication and playfulness creates closeness in an intimate relationship.* Remember the days of innocent youth when time stood still and you giggled and shared intimate visions of grandeur with the cute guy you were dating? Perhaps this moment can be recaptured, but through the lens of emotional maturity. A bridge to deeper connection and emotional intimacy is realized when you share your thoughts, dreams, fears, aspirations, and vulnerabilities. Sharing laughter at our foibles and frailties makes each partner appreciate that the other is *genuinely human and beautifully imperfect.* Kidding around with each other in a kind and supportive way can defuse most situations and bring an element of playfulness into the relationship.

- *Verbalizing feelings of love, expressing gratitude, and offering words of affirmation also contribute to emotional intimacy.* Words and actions are essential for expressing love, affection, and appreciation. Regular and heartfelt communication nurtures the emotional connection and reinforces the love between partners. Sometimes the smallest gesture can have the greatest impact on how someone feels. No one willing walks on a tightrope of vulnerability without a safety net of emotional support from their partner. If we want a deeper relationship, we need to do our part.

We know effective communication skills are essential for building healthy and fulfilling relationships, so let's visit some basic tenets as a refresher. I've been in sales and coaching for many years and the one thing I was taught when I ventured into the profession of selling is you have two ears and one mouth for a reason.

"It takes much more than just hearing to listen intentionally, mindfully, and thoughtfully."

We all like to feel heard—to feel as if what we're saying matters to those we care about. To help facilitate this within a relationship give your partner the full attention he deserves and seek to understand his perspective without interrupting or formulating a response before he's done speaking.

Most people will raise their hand and say they're good listeners, but *active listening* is harder than we make think. If we're honest with ourselves, we all tend to interrupt people as they're talking because we're anxious to share our perspective. After all, we believe we have the answer, which will shorten the discussion . . . we're simply trying to be "helpful." A better approach, however, is to show interest through non-verbal cues, such as maintaining eye contact and nodding, and providing verbal feedback to demonstrate and validate your understanding.

There is a distinct difference between how men and women communicate. We women are typically more emotionally expressive. We love to share our ideas and thoughts and seek to feel supported and comforted in return. Whereas men as a standard rule are more pragmatic. They like to fix things and solve problems. It's helpful in a relationship for both parties to express thoughts, feelings, and needs clearly and directly, using simple and concise language. It's funny, but I've heard many men say that words women use like *always* or *never* drive them to distraction. They're blanket statements that indicate no exceptions exist and there's no path forward for a resolution—they can't fix anything. To bridge the difference in styles, it's helpful when men and women process their feelings together, ensuring both walk away feeling heard and understood.

Seek to understand and *empathize* with the other person's emotions and experiences. Try to put yourself in their shoes so you can try to appreciate how they're feeling, even if you may not agree with their perspective. Think back on times when you immediately dismissed or "dissed" how someone felt because it didn't align with your thought process. What happened? More than likely, it caused a defensive response and shut down any real communication. To really understand each other we must be willing to hear what the other person thinks and feels–giving space for open expression.

Think about your body language, tone of voice, and facial expressions. Ensure they align with your intended message and convey openness, respect, and attentiveness. This is something that you'll explore throughout the relationship. I've walked into the room and felt a cold shoulder from Mark. I may think he's upset with me, whereas he's just focused and completely baffled by my interpretation of his *body language.*

How we provide feedback is key. Too often, we stack our emotions–being resentful or frustrated because things are left unresolved. Another similar situation comes up and we add another layer to our emotional stack. Soon, we look for reasons to validate our negative feelings about someone or a situation (this is especially true if we've not reconciled our past). We hear ourselves saying, "See, I knew it," or "You never can…." Respectful feedback that focuses on specific behaviors or situations is always more constructive than allowing things to fester. Stacking lessens our control and often our ability to hit the pause button. Use "I" statements to express your feelings and avoid blaming or criticizing. Statements like, "You're such a …" versus, "Your *behavior* is so . . ." will be received very differently. You're not throwing the entire person under the proverbial bus, but rather an action they demonstrated. There's room for improvement rather than feeling like you've condemned their entire being. This may seem like a nuance, but the impact is anything but subtle.

Seek clarification when needed to ensure there's mutual understanding. Summarize the main points of the conversation to confirm that you are both on the same page. This is especially important when you're dealing with a conflict. Both partners should be willing to find a mutually beneficial solution and, potentially, a path forward that will help to minimize the number of future occurrences.

Choose an appropriate time and place for important conversations. Things that are important to discuss deserve to be given the right time and place so both of you are focused. Having a sensitive discussion following a bottle of wine and night cap may not be good timing. Just a thought … a shot of courage has led to many lover's quarrels. It's helpful to agree that tabling a conversation is often healthier than pushing through.

One of the many things for which we can all be grateful is the diversity that surrounds us. But we should try to be aware of ***cultural differences*** in communication styles and norms. If possible, adapt to the cultural context of the person with whom you're communicating to foster understanding and avoid misunderstandings. If you're able to show respect for their differences it will help you to cross the cultural divide that may initially exist.

Without question, effective communication and emotional intimacy require active effort and practice. It means being present, listening with empathy, and expressing yourself honestly and respectfully. But the reciprocal gift you'll enjoy is immense. By honing these skills, you can enhance your relationships, resolve conflicts more effectively, and foster deeper connections with people in your life.

Emotional intimacy is built over time through trust, vulnerability, and open communication. *It requires both partners to actively invest in nurturing the emotional connection.* Embrace the opportunity to cultivate emotional intimacy in your relationships as a mature woman and enjoy the depth and richness it can bring to your life.

EMOTIONAL CONNECTIONS

Embracing vulnerability and sharing emotional intimacy are such important topics, that I've outlined several suggested exercises. These exercises will help you to discover whether there are areas you still need to work on as you explore finding love again.

Self-reflection:

Find a quiet and comfortable space where you can reflect and write without distractions. Take a few deep breaths to center yourself. If you do Yoga breathing that's perfect. Begin by asking a few open-ended questions about your beliefs and assumptions. Allow yourself to be freely expressive without judgment. Write as much as you need in your journal to fully explore your thoughts. This is a discovery process to help you uncover areas that may be holding you back. Here are some questions, but you'll intuitively know what questions to ask yourself that will serve you, but here's a starting point:

- What are my expectations for a healthy and fulfilling relationship?
- What do I believe about my own worthiness for love and respect?
- How do I view communication and conflict resolution in a partnership? How well have I navigated issues in the past? What have I learned that will be beneficial?
- What are my beliefs about trust and loyalty in a relationship?
- Do I have limiting beliefs or fears that may impact my ability to fully engage in a new relationship?
- How do I perceive vulnerability and emotional intimacy in a partnership?
- What are beliefs about personal boundaries and the importance of individual autonomy within a relationship?

Innately we realize the influence our upbringing, cultural background, and past experiences have had on shaping our beliefs and assumptions. When we're young we collect impressions that define what we consider normal as an adult. When we become consciously aware about what we watch and who we listen to we can curate these impressions. Think about the messages you received from family, friends, media, and society. Reflect on any significant events or relationships that may have influenced your beliefs–both positive and negative. We all have an opportunity to revisit, edit, and unlearn past impressions. When you are young choices are made for you. The choices turn into impressions. As an adult you can make your own choices *and* impressions: You can rewrite your stories.

Take a hard look at your beliefs and assumptions. Ask yourself if they are serving you well or if they may be limiting your potential for growth and happiness. Are there any beliefs that are outdated or ones that no longer align with your values?

Echo chambers of common thought don't help us to grow–they may seem comfortable as your position is always validated. But it's much more fun and enlightening to engage in conversations with individuals who possess different beliefs and perspectives. This can help broaden our understanding and challenge any biases or assumptions we may hold and not even realize. Some of the most grounded, and interesting, people I know read and learn voraciously. Whether its books, articles, podcasts, seminars– they always seek to expand their minds and discover different perspectives. Differences that they can learn from and integrate into their lives.

Think about specific situations or relationships where your beliefs and assumptions may have influenced your thoughts, feelings, and actions. This may seem like a broad question but consider whether for example your first husband fulfilled someone else's definition of the "ideal" partner or whether a career choice was influenced by past impressions of what success looked like. These are just a couple of typical examples but think about it. Consider whether these influential beliefs were helpful or if they hindered your ability to navigate certain life experiences more effectively.

We don't realize, I didn't realize, how many actions I've taken in my life based on someone else's scripting. Like when we honored our past, we can take things from the people and events that have influenced our impressions regarding what *we now feel* align with who we are and the life we're designing.

Like most steps in our personal development journeys, this is not a "one and done" exercise. As you grow and explore your beliefs and impressions things will change. You'll discover a new lens like I've mentioned in prior chapters. Regularly revisit your beliefs and assumptions as you gain new insights and experiences. Be open to revisiting and updating them as needed. Give yourself the gift to embrace a growth mindset that allows for personal evolution and learning. If, upon reflection, you are quick to condemn past actions and mistakes you'll shut down your ability to grow. Our minds gravitate to pleasure and avoid pain. We need to encourage and celebrate our power to reflect, assess, and choose.

Remember, this exercise is *your journey of self-discovery and self-awareness.* This is a present you're giving yourself when you approach it with curiosity, compassion, and a willingness to challenge and grow beyond your existing beliefs and assumptions.

A SUGGESTED EXERCISE FRAMEWORK

MY BELIEFS OR ASSUMPTIONS	HOW HAVE THEY SERVED ME?

*"When you know yourself you are empowered. When
you accept yourself you are invincible."*
—Tina Lifford

Mindfulness and Emotional Awareness: As you go along, practice mindfulness and emotional awareness exercises on your own. This involves *tuning into* your emotions, observing them without judgment, and exploring their underlying causes. Be curious. By developing a greater awareness of your own emotions, you can better communicate and connect with your partner on a deeper emotional level.

In this chapter, we covered a lot of insightful topics building from the self-reflection and personal development goals realized in the prior chapters. A solid foundation of self-confidence and authenticity will allow you to embrace vulnerability more openly over time.

It's as important to establish and communicate your boundaries as it is to understand your beliefs and assumptions, your life impressions. All these steps are valuable steppingstones when opening your heart to love again. We explored the ways and reasons why communicating honestly and sharing your fears, dreams, aspirations and needs helps to foster trust in a relationship. We discussed patterns and emotional triggers and the value of pausing between the stimuli and your response rather than simply reacting.

In chapter seven, we will focus on how to nurture a healthy relationship. Although you may not yet be in a relationship, I would encourage you to still review this chapter in preparation for finding love again. If you have embarked on dating and exploring a new relationship this chapter will give you some guidance and food for thought.

BALANCING ACT

Nurturing Healthy Relationships While Honoring Yourself

"I'm not a one in a million kinda girl. I'm a once in a lifetime kind of woman."

- JAY SHETTY

Perhaps you've found someone who shares your values and you've started a nice relationship – *congratulations!* Sharing love is one of life's greatest gifts. No matter how strong its foundation, any relationship without nurturing will eventually struggle. A healthy relationship requires putting in the time, attention and love needed to strengthen the partnership. To truly work and flourish, relationships should be given daily attention. I think this need becomes heightened as we get older given our baggage and emotional triggers (which we're working through together). It seemed easier when we were younger. Our expectations were not as high as we lived more in the moment, the future seemed infinite and the risks were rarely considered. At this stage of our lives, we want to take a more defined and refined approach. There are some habits that will help you nurture your relationship. Stephen Covey says that love is a verb: *We choose to love.* It's a conscious decision and one that requires conscious effort.

As you might anticipate, good communication is key to enjoying a healthy relationship. We touched on this in great detail in the proceeding chapter, but it bears repeating. Through open communication, you create a *safe space* for discussing issues when they arise. Rather than pointing fingers or making excuses, both parties can practice the *art* of conflict resolution. *It's not about who's right or who is wrong, but rather learning about each other.* And assuming responsibility and apologizing when appropriate.

Which brings us back to active listening. I've watched couples, and I've been guilty of this behavior, who don't really listen to what the other person is saying. We're often so quick to defend our position or say our piece that we don't let the other person finish what they have to say. This behavior makes the other person feel figuratively and literally unheard, which is frustrating and undermines our trust to openly share our thoughts and feelings.

Showing appreciation for the big and small things your partner does for you every day sounds simple. But it's so easy for us to take each other for granted over time. He's a great guy, and may be naturally giving, but no one wants to feel unappreciated. Think about how you can show gratitude for your partner's efforts, qualities, and actions. Small gestures of kindness and acknowledgement can go a long way in nurturing a healthy relationship. I would encourage you to regularly express your love and gratitude to your partner, making him feel valued and cherished. I'm not talking about a one-sided relationship, but what I have found when dealing with "good" men is that they will step up and emulate the behaviors you demonstrate. I love the movie *As Good as It Gets* with Jack Nicholson. Here's this quirky man with all sorts of emotional baggage, but he makes a comment to Helen Hunt, "You make me want to become a better man." It's a movie, but don't underestimate the power of this statement and its reality outside of Hollywood.

When you and your partner both feel appreciated, it will nurture your relationship. Nothing undermines a relationship faster than one person feeling like they are not appreciated or valued. Simply saying "thank you" can speak volumes.

I love the old saying, "Forgiveness is a divine." I would add, it's a gift that keeps giving. Psychologists generally define forgiveness as a conscious, deliberate decision to release feelings of resentment or vengeance toward a person. Get into the habit of forgiving your partner when you've talked through a problem when he was at fault. Each partner has his/her nuances and flaws, but I would say that women have more of a tendency to bring up past trespasses when convenient. It can become a weapon that we wield against our men. Practice the art of forgiveness and let go of resolved conflicts. It's healthy for the relationship and it's healthy for you.

A wonderful and highly acclaimed book that captured the attention of many is called *Men Are from Mars, Women are from Venus*.[16] This book focuses on the language of love; the different ways people express their love. Although we may speak different love languages, acts of service or giving is universal and one of the most important acts you can do in a relationship. Recognize what is most important to your partner or find something he doesn't like to do. Take over this responsibility for a bit to give him a break.

This goes both ways. Acts of service are a great way to show your partner you care about your relationship.

When we were younger, perhaps we were more inclined to be defined by love. But now we know the value of our personal interests and passions; the need to remain true to your authentic self. One of the things that attracts us to a partner is how interesting we find them. Pursuing individual passions, interests, hobbies, and goals helps to keep the spark. Encourage your partner to do the same. This allows you both to grow and maintain a healthy sense of self, which ultimately contributes to a stronger partnership. You bring back into the relationship outside interests and experiences that differ from those of your partner.

This naturally leads us to the importance of being each other's cheerleader by encouraging and supporting your partner's personal growth and aspirations. Provide a safe space for you both to explore your passions and dreams. Celebrate your achievements and be there for each other during challenging times. Supporting each other's growth fosters a true sense of partnership and mutual respect.

Although it's important to maintain our own interests and friendships, investing time together is paramount–it's all about building shared memories. Be intentional with the time and actions you share with your partner. Carve out time that is dedicated "together time." Perhaps it's a weekly date night, going for a walk, playing a sport together like tennis, pickleball, or golf. It's about choosing activities that you both enjoy and can share on a consistent basis. It's an act of demonstration that you both prioritize your relationship.

Keeping romance alive should be fun! A Time Magazine article highlighted studies that indicated that laughing is good for the soul. "But we now know something else: Sharing giggles with a romantic partner keeps the lovey-dovey feelings going, according to a study published in the *Journal of Personal Relationships*. It seems common sense to say that people who laugh together are probably happier together, and that happier couples would have a longer, healthier, more vital relationship. In the next chapter we'll delve into why having fun and becoming playfully childish sometimes is so good for a relationship, and for ourselves. Surprise each other with small gestures of love and affection.

How do you express love? Intimacy and physical touch go together. As humans, we crave, we need, human contact. This can be done in a variety of ways such as hugging, kissing, holding hands, snuggling, and yes, sex. Most men, even as they age, maintain their testosterone levels, albeit perhaps at a lower level for some. A healthy sex life is important for a man's self-esteem … and it's pleasurable. Intimacy is not just physical, but emotional. It cultivates a deeper sense of connection. It's also a trust thing. We are most vulnerable when we're naked with another person. We don't need to be perfect. I've spoken with so many women who don't feel good about how they look. You really have two choices. Improve how you look through exercise and diet or accept the way you look. Keeping yourself cloistered from sharing intimacy doesn't seem like an ideal third choice. Self-confidence is sexy and doesn't always need to be paired with a flawless physique. One perfect example of this was a woman I knew many years ago. She was on my sales team and honestly was not attractive and was very overweight. But she carried herself with such confidence and poise. She dressed well and conveyed a sensual appeal that drew many men to her. It was about her persona not the perfection of how she looked. As women, we're typically much harsher on ourselves. Going back to what we talked about in an earlier chapter, live from the inside out.

Nurturing a healthy relationship is a shared effort, one that will be unique to you and your partner. It's important to communicate openly and honestly, respect each other's boundaries, and prioritize the well-being and growth of you both. By investing time, effort, and love into the relationship, you can create a strong and fulfilling partnership, one that hopefully stands the test of time.

EXPRESS LOVE AUTHENTICALLY

INDIVIDUAL EXERCISES

Journaling and meditation *are* wonderful accompanying exercises to nurture your relationship. You'll see I've outlined different ways you can focus your meditative practice to get you started. Where focus goes energy flows. The hope is that you've found someone worthy of a shared relationship. These exercises are to help you feel grounded and focused on what's possible.

- ***Gratitude journaling:*** Set aside a few minutes each day to write down things about which you are grateful in your relationship. This practice helps shift your focus to the positive aspects and cultivates a sense of appreciation. As Stephen Covey would say, "Love is a verb"–we choose to love someone. We spoke about gratitude earlier and that we typically want to please those that we love. If we feel appreciated for demonstrating certain actions, we're more likely to cultivate and demonstrate these actions.

- ***Relationship reflections:*** Use journaling as a tool to reflect on your relationship. Write about your experiences, challenges, and growth within the relationship. This can help you gain insights, identify patterns, and set intentions for improvement. It can also illuminate the positives.

- ***Love letters:*** Write heartfelt letters to your partner expressing your love, admiration, and appreciation. This exercise allows you to reflect on your feelings and communicate them in a meaningful way. Cards are another nice way to show a man that you care. One thing *I've realized over time is that good men who are emotional healthy are the men who strive to become better versions of themselves for the woman they love.* Please read that again. Women hold the power, not in a bad or manipulative way, but we are genetically wired to nurture greater depth within a relationship. If we show our love and respect, respect is key, a good man will feel encouraged and safe to demonstrate their vulnerability and love in return.

- ***Mindful meditation:*** Incorporate mindfulness meditation into your routine to cultivate presence and awareness about your relationship. Set aside a few minutes each day to focus on your breath, observe your thoughts and emotions, and feel a sense of compassion towards yourself *and* your partner. I think this is especially important if you've not been in a relationship for some time. It helps to keep you focused on the here and now versus the past. The fear of being hurt or disappointed or the fear that he'll find out you're not as wonderful as he now believes. These insecurities or fears will undermine what could be a nice, budding relationship. We all have fears and have experienced imposter syndrome, but conscious meditation and journaling helps us to navigate to the other side where we feel more empowered and embrace our self-worth. The other side when we acknowledge that we've grown and that vulnerability is not something to fear, but something we're willing to explore with the right person.
- ***Loving-kindness meditation:*** Practice loving-kindness meditation by sending well wishes and positive energy to your partner. Visualize them happy, healthy, and loved. This meditation helps foster feelings of love, empathy, and connection.
- ***Reflective meditation:*** Use meditation as a time for self-reflection on your role in the relationship. Explore your own emotions, reactions, and behaviors, and consider how they impact the dynamics between you and your partner.

Journaling and meditation are personal practices, so feel free to adapt them to your own preferences and needs. They can provide valuable insights, promote self-awareness, and enhance your overall well-being, which in turn will have a tremendous impact on your relationships—and your life.

PARTNER EXERCISES

As you review these exercises, please give yourself space to pause and see how you feel when you read through them. Do these exercises feel comfortable and natural? Some may not feel natural but would still be helpful. Others may not feel natural because you still have some personal growth to experience. I'd encourage you to integrate some semblance of what is outlined naturally into your relationship to get to know each other on a much deeper level.

Sharing gratitude: Take turns expressing gratitude for each other. Share specific things you appreciate about your partner and how they contribute to your life. This exercise fosters a sense of appreciation and deepens emotional connection. It also helps your partner to realize those characteristics and behaviors about which you're most grateful. This doesn't need to feel like a *formal session* but adding gratitude to a relationship can be powerful.

Vulnerability practice: This can involve sharing personal stories, fears, or dreams that you may not have shared before. Start with small steps and gradually build up to deeper levels of vulnerability. At the risk of repeating myself again, we're all flawed. We all have made huge mistakes (defined by our definition of success) and we have things about which we're enormously embarrassed. I'm not suggesting that you put everything on the table and take or leave it, but over time, you'll both feel more confident and comfortable sharing more of yourselves. This means that you've established a deep sense of trust and respect. Understanding someone deeply allows us to be supportive and loving–despite their flaws or, perhaps, because they're flawed. Beauty is often found in our imperfections. It's what makes us unique and special.

Emotional check-ins: Set aside regular times to check in with each other emotionally. Create a safe and non-judgmental space where you can openly share your feelings, concerns, and joys. This exercise promotes open communication and strengthens emotional intimacy. Life can be complicated, and it helps to consciously make time to talk, to check-in. To discuss what's working and what's not. What can you do together to foster an even stronger relationship? How are you both feeling? The stability that comes from knowing where you stand is huge! It's not a, "Let's talk," moment. It's a positive investment of time and attention in building a strong foundation from which you both grow together.

Writing love letters: Take the time to write heartfelt love letters or cards to your partner. Express your deepest emotions, appreciation, and love for them. This exercise allows you to tap into your emotions and communicate them in a thoughtful and intimate way. It fosters emotional connection and vulnerability.

Active listening: When communicating, practice active listening. Give each other your full attention, maintain eye contact, and show genuine interest in what they're saying. Reflect their thoughts and feelings back to them to ensure understanding. This exercise enhances empathy and deepens emotional connection. It also helps to ensure you truly understand what was said and, if not, give your partner time to clarify their point. So often, we make assumptions based on our own experiences rather than listening to what someone else may be saying.

In this chapter we talked a lot about how to nurture your relationship. How to move beyond feeling unsteady and vulnerable to really connecting with your partner by being authentic and curious. With a strong sense of self-worth, we can become more openly expressive of our feelings and see things in the present context. Next, we're going to explore the connection between intimacy and having fun together.

THE JOYFULL BOND

Cultivating Laughter for Deeper Connection and Intimacy

"Laughter is the language of the soul."

- PABLO NERUDA

Have you ever wondered whether you've become too serious? Do you marvel at the innocence of children and how easily their giggles fill the air? If we're not careful, we can lose that unbridled enthusiasm for simple pleasures that used to bring us joy. Life's difficulties have taken their toll, and we find ourselves laughing at certain jokes or on occasion with friends, but we've lost the innocence of laughter; the ability to laugh at ourselves and be willing to get silly.

Laughter is the best medicine; an adage that still rings true. What is also true is that laughter shared with a partner brings you closer. *Joyful laughter is often considered to be the universal language that brings people together and forges lasting relationships.* Taking it one step further, laughter can help cultivate intimacy and closeness in romantic relationships. Research suggests that sharing laughter with your beau can profoundly enhance the overall quality of your relationship.

Before we delve into this further, I'd like to ask that you step back and consider when you were younger and how silly you could get with friends and boyfriends. You'd tease each other, make fun of silly things, and cultivate a shared creed of funny sayings and life experiences.

So, what is the appeal of acting youthful and carefree when we talk about dating? It's one of the reasons men state as far as why they have a hang-up about dating women their age. We have our own hang-ups, perhaps about men our age, but likely for different reasons. One thing I've heard from mature men (nice guys) is that they feel many older women have lost the ease of laughter and the casualness of life. I know this is a generalization, so I'm not saying this applies to every man or women, but it's something to think about. Life is complicated and our world has become more complex. Laughter and silliness bring levity and allow moments of unbridled innocence to reign.

Dating below our age is fine for both men and women but we should take into consideration the appeal of doing this. Most of us want to enjoy the benefit of wisdom and life experiences without feeling old. We enjoy being with people who can touch that youthful side of our personalities.

Whether it's spraying someone with a hose when they're not expecting it or teasing a man by running around the house in a sexy outfit. There are so many ways you can introduce frivolous fun into a mature relationship. Laughing hysterically together based on something you both saw or some foolish act one of you did at the expense of the other person's laughter–is healthy! You can be nutty and mature.

When we become stronger and more comfortable in our own skin and have cultivated a healthy level of self-worth, we can laugh at ourselves without becoming defensive. We have a strong core of self-love, so we feel more empowered to simply *let go.* None of us are perfect so trying to act as if we are can be exhausting and can feel like a protective shield to a prospective partner, because it comes across as if you're not willing to let people in.

Whether you're working or retired, our world today seems more stressful. *Laughter is a wonderful way to reduce stress.* Laughter triggers endorphins in our body. It's natures feel-good hormone. The shared experience of reducing stress and unwinding through laughter helps couples be more present together and engaged with each other.

Studies have indicated that relationships where laughter is regularly shared score higher on the satisfaction scale. Laughter creates mutual memories and bonds that foster heightened fulfillment. By regularly sharing laughter you strengthen the emotional connection with your partner, which brings you both back to the enjoyable aspects of your relationship, which can help reduce conflicts. As a result, you learn how to diffuse tension and instill a more positive outlook overall.

Like when you felt more carefree (a personal choice), laughter can create a couple's ritual or creed, if you will. It establishes a special connection. Whether it's a comedy show that you both enjoy, a certain phrase or word that you find amusing, or engaging in playful banter, moments of shared laughter create a routine and stronger bond, which then become cherished memories.

Have you ever found yourself in a stressful situation and someone cracks a joke? You both laughed before refocusing on the issue at hand.

Laughter can also be a potent tool for building trust. The ability to laugh together even when things get tough demonstrates an ability to navigate difficulties as a team. There is strength in the ability to share humor as it builds trust and establishes a relationship where both people feel safe and supported.

Laughter is also integral to effective communication as it can help break down barriers. When laughter is a natural part of a relationship individuals feel safe expressing themselves more openly. In turn, couples connect at a deeper level of understanding … again building a stronger emotional bond.

And let's not forget the tremendous benefit laughter has on our physicality. According to the Mayo Clinic, laughter stimulates many organs in our body. It enhances your intake of oxygen-rich air, stimulates your heart, lungs, and muscles and increases endorphins that are released in your brain. The endorphins released during laughter help to reduce the effect of cortisol, which when present for prolonged periods of time due to stress, puts you at a higher risk of a host of health problems like heart disease, high blood pressure, and diabetes. There you have it. – *Laughter is the best medicine!*

Smiling is another amazingly simple way to decrease your stress and strengthen your immune system. It improves your mood, and it can help increase your positivity. Many studies have indicated the emotional value of smiling. Your smile connects directly to your nervous system and brain, so smiling *can* improve your mood. After all, it's difficult to be sad or stressed when you're smiling like Jim Carrey.

Smiling easily and sharing joyful laughter are
healthy for you and your relationship.

CHAPTER NINE

REFLECTIONS AND REVELATIONS

A Recap of Our Journey

"Every positive thought is a silent prayer that will change your life."

— JAY SHETTY

hope by reading this book and going through the various exercises you now understand and appreciate that falling in love with yourself is the starting point for your journey to finding love again. By becoming a better version of yourself you will become open to attracting the type of man you seek. An investment in yourself is well worth the effort.

The aging process can be liberating. Fall in love with your uniqueness! Become more accepting of your flaws and quirks. Statements like, "I've always been this way," don't help us to grow. Assuming responsibility for your uniqueness means you appreciate the imperfections that serve you and understand which imperfections limit you. It's about taking control of who you are and who you're becoming on your self-defined journey. Self-worth is empowering as it frees us from the burden of striving to be someone we're not. We give ourselves permission to be authentic and live life passionately. Let's promise together that this is just the beginning.

It was Stephen Covey who first introduced me to the concept of an emotional bank account. He explains the concept of an emotional bank account with a metaphor. "By proactively doing things that builds trust in a relationship, one makes deposits." It's a wonderful concept for any relationship, whether family, friends, or business associates, but even more powerful if used to build self-trust. A woman who sacrifices her needs for everyone else is likely to become depleted, exhausted, and bitter. Making deposits into your emotional bank account allows you to get stronger. We start believing in ourselves. We feel proud about what we're accomplishing and who we're becoming. We move away from perfectionism and external measurements of self-worth to acceptance and growth. It's a beautiful journey.

Self-acceptance allows you to show up authentically and confidently in relationships. It moves us away from seeking self-love elsewhere. Intimate relationships can often become unbalanced if we need that person to make us feel whole or happy. Your core principles or North Star should guide your life's purpose and keep you centered. If you've lost a part of yourself through life's journey, now is the time to reclaim your self-worth and, ultimately, your happiness. You shouldn't settle. You deserve to embrace life more fully. As my mother would often say, "This isn't a dress rehearsal."

Sharing love from a place of authenticity strengthens the bonds we're able to establish with others, whether it's with romantic partners, family members, or friends. We're able to foster trust, intimacy, and connection, creating a deeper sense of belonging and support.

When we learn from the past and live from the inside-out, we give ourselves the opportunity to be liberated from self-defeating beliefs. For example, if you believe *all the good men are taken*, because that's just what people say, you'll automatically believe that anyone not "taken" is no good. By grounding ourselves through a path of personal development and self-reflection we "see" more clearly. We don't superimpose false narratives on the present. We've dealt with our past and are now able to use our guided intuition to make decisions that serve us.

When we're able to share love authentically, we cultivate empathy and compassion for others. It allows us to understand and relate to their experiences, leading to greater understanding, tolerance, and kindness. This can create a ripple effect, inspiring others to also share love and kindness.

Love is an elixir of life. Expressing love and receiving love releases feel-good hormones like oxytocin (without all the health issues), which can elevate your mood, reduce stress, and increase overall happiness.

Sharing love encourages personal growth and self-discovery. It challenges us to be vulnerable, open-hearted, and compassionate. By giving and receiving love, we learn more about ourselves, our values, and *our capacity to love*. This can lead to a greater sense of purpose, fulfillment, and personal development.

Ultimately, sharing love has the power to create a positive impact not only in our own lives but also in the lives of those around us. It fosters happiness, strengthens relationships, and contributes to a more compassionate and connected world.

Learning how to accept and love ourselves more authentically is a journey. Be patient and give yourself grace and know you are worth it!

A quote that has inspired my continued growth is, "Love is a gift, one better shared." Before I met Mark, my life was full of friends and activities and personal passions. I didn't need a man to define or complete me. My years of self-development had instilled a deep sense of gratitude and appreciation for the woman I had become. My relationship was additive, it introduced a richer depth to my life. By sharing my mind, body, and soul with a healthy and grounded man who cherishes, loves, and respects me, imperfections and all, this expanded the aperture through which I experience life.

It has been my privilege to have the opportunity to serve you. My heartfelt hope for everyone who has ventured down this path with me, is to find authentic love again—for yourself and a future partner.

The secret to living a fulfilling life is trusting your instincts, staying true to your values, and chasing after what your heart wants.

ABOUT THE AUTHOR AND SELF-WORTH FOUNDATIONS

Jacqueline is a passionate advocate for women's empowerment, driven by the belief that every woman can achieve her purpose in life and business. Her journey of having lived on four continents fostered an adventurous spirit and a deep curiosity about life's possibilities, shaping her into a visionary thinker who inspires and guides her clients toward their own breakthroughs.

As a dynamic entrepreneur, artist, and business executive, Jacqueline has been a prominent figure in the personal development and coaching industries for over 15 years. Her commitment to excellence has led her to study alongside the luminaries of the personal development industry, equipping her with the tools to navigate her personal and professional challenges and reach her full potential.

Jacqueline's heartfelt desire to serve others inspired her to author Anchor Your Self-Worth, a transformative guide that empowers women to embrace authenticity and rediscover their life's purpose. Through a guided journey of self-discovery, she invites her readers to anchor their self-worth and ignite their passion.

SELF-WORTH FOUNDATIONS: EMPOWER PERSONAL AND PROFESSIONAL GROWTH

At Self-Worth Foundations, we believe that self-worth and authenticity are the cornerstones of a fulfilling life. Our mission is to empower individuals with personal clarity and confidence as they navigate their personal and professional journeys.

We offer a range of online classes and personalized coaching services designed to support personal development and entrepreneurial success. Our programs emphasize the importance of a clear sense of purpose, strong direction, and an unwavering belief in one's inherent worthiness of success. Without a solid foundation of self-worth, even the most robust business plans can falter.

Our holistic approach focuses on nurturing personal strengths and developing enduring skills that are integral to both professional achievements and personal satisfaction. Through our coaching services, available in small group settings or one-on-one sessions, we provide tailored support and guidance. Each participant receives a personalized roadmap to help them achieve their distinct goals, ensuring they have the necessary tools and confidence to realize their potential.

You can find out more about our services at
www.selfworthfoundations.com

REFERENCE

1   *The Artist's Way*, Julia Cameron

2   **Dr. Joe Dispenza:** https://www.youtube.com/watch?v=GbbZ-9Jjq90

3   Stanford's Laura Carstensen: https://www.wbur.org/
    onpoint/2021/04/02/science-older-happier-study-pandemic

4   *The 7 Habits of Highly Effective People*, Stephen Covey

5   **John Hopkins Study:** https://www.hopkinsmedicine.org/health/
    wellness-and-prevention/forgiveness-your-health-depends-on-it

6   **Psychology Today:** Psychology Today https://www.
    psychologytoday.com/us/blog/quantum-leaps/201907/
    how-rewrite-your-past-narrative

7   **Tony Robbins:** https://www.tonyrobbins.com/date-with-destiny/
    how-to-change-your-life-with-just-one-simple-story/?utm_source=
    linkedIn&utm_medium=social&utm_campaign=Change%20
    Your%20Life

8   **Tom Rowland**

9   **American Psychology Association**: https://dictionary.apa.org/self-love

10 **Mayo Clinic** - Mindfulness

11 **Brain & Behavior:** https://bbrfoundation.org/blog/
    self-love-and-what-it-means#:~:text=People%20who%20have%20
    more%20self,%2C%20and%20lessen%20self%2Dlove.

12 **Entrepreneur:** https://www.entrepreneur.com/living/9-ways-to-attract-good-energy-today-and-every-day/332544

13 **Psychology Today**: https://www.psychologytoday.com/us/blog/click-here-happiness/202201/4-ways-know-your-worth

14 *Dare to Lead*, Brené Brown

15 **Psychology Today**: https://www.psychologytoday.com/us/blog/the-gen-y-psy/201810/how-spot-your-emotional-triggers

16 *Men Are From Mars, Women Are From Venus,* John Gray

www.ingramcontent.com/pod-product-compliance
Lightning Source LLC
Chambersburg PA
CBHW071550120726
48009CB00007B/248/J